A Lady's Ranch Life
in Montana

D1435215

The Western Frontier Library

A Lady's Ranch Life in Montana

By Isabel F. Randall

Edited by Richard L. Saunders
Foreword by Shirley A. Leckie

University of Oklahoma Press : Norman

Also by Richard L. Saunders

Glimpses of Wonderland: The Haynes and Their Postcards of Yellowstone National Park, 1899–1967 (Bozeman, 1997)

Printing in Deseret: Mormons, Politics, Economy, and Utah's Incunabula, 1849–1851 (Salt Lake City, 2001)

The Yellowstone Reader: The National Park in Popular Fiction, Folklore, and Verse (Salt Lake City, 2003)

This book is published with the generous assistance of The McCasland Foundation, Duncan, Oklahoma.

Library of Congress Cataloging-in-Publication Data

I. R. (Isabelle Randall)
   A lady's ranch life in Montana / by Isabel F. Randall ; edited by Richard L. Saunders ; foreword by Shirley A. Leckie.
      p.   cm. — (The Western frontier library ; 67)
   Includes bibliographical references (p.   ) and index.
   ISBN 0-8061-3609-X (alk. paper) — ISBN 0-8061-3640-5 (pbk. : alk. paper)
   1. I. R. (Isabelle Randall) 2. Women ranchers—Montana—Biography. 3. Ranchers—Montana—Biography. 4. English—Montana—Biography. 5. Ranch life—Montana. 6. Montana—Social life and customs—19th century. 7. Montana—Biography. I. Title: Lady's ranche life in Montana. II. Saunders, Richard L., 1963– III. Title. IV. Series.

F731.R18 2004
978.6'02'092—dc22
[B]

                                                    2004041209

A Lady's Ranch Life in Montana is Volume 67 in The Western Frontier Library.

1 2 3 4 5 6 7 8 9 10

A newly-married couple might go [to the West] with the certainty of doing well, provided they had suitable means to make a good beginning; the wife would everywhere be treated with the greatest respect, and with moderately good management need never be subject to any special discomforts.

William Saunders,
Through the Light Continent; or,
The United States in 1877–8

Contents

Illustrations

Foreword

When twenty-four-year-old Englishwoman Isabel Fitz-Herbert Randall arrived in southwestern Montana in 1884, she was a newlywed. She and her husband, James L. Randall, five years her senior, expected to reap a fortune in the American West by raising horses and through James Randall's investment and participation in the Moreland Ranch Stock Company. In her quest for economic advancement, Isabel was similar to many native-born Americans who were moving westward and many immigrants from various parts of Europe who were settling in the northwestern United States in hopes of achieving a better future for their families.

As Richard L. Saunders explains in his introduction to this new edition of Isabel Randall's *A Lady's Ranche Life in Montana,* first published in 1887, many in the United States and the British Isles, during the 1880s, thought that the quickest way to riches was by grazing livestock on the U.S. public range. Certainly, James S. Brisbin's best-selling

The Beef Bonanza promised profits of 25 percent annually for stocking cattle on U.S. land and 35 percent for stocking sheep. As for raising horses, Brisbin advised ranchers to mix high-quality stallions with wild mares to earn a profit of 25 to 33 percent per annum.[1] His projections and those of others as well attracted so many ranchers to the western states and territories that the range was fast becoming overstocked. In addition the Chicago market for beef would soon be oversupplied, and the weather in the West was due to revert to periods of drought in the summers and severe cold in the winters. In one of her letters, Isabel stated a comforting myth when she wrote that as more settlers moved into Montana the winter weather would become milder, since this pattern had supposedly unfolded elsewhere in the West. She did not know that vast numbers of ranchers, hoping to capitalize on the ranching boom, would soon face huge financial and personal losses. Isabel and James Randall may have recouped their initial investment in the Moreland Ranch Stock Company, but they would have nothing to show after five years of hard labor in Montana's Gallatin Valley. Moreover, they would not be welcomed back. Their former neighbors were incensed after reading *A Lady's Ranche Life in Montana,* which they found insulting and demeaning.

On the surface, as a daughter of the gentry in England, Isabel should have experienced few problems in incorporating herself into American life. Certainly, her aspirations and experiences were similar to those of most American women in the West. Moving westward, even as late as the 1880s, was for most wives and mothers a step backward in time in terms of housekeeping. A rural setting left them without urban conveniences and amenities and often deprived of the companionship of other women. The round of chores, which included making butter, tending gardens, and caring for animals such as pigs and chickens, only added to the usual burden of ongoing domestic duties within the home. Loneliness and drudgery were common complaints in the West, and another was failure "to get ahead." By the late 1880s a popular song in America was "Starving to Death on My Government Claim."[2] Still— whatever the hardships and disappointments—many women, like many men, embraced the chance to live in the trans-Mississippi West as a way of advancing their family's fortunes.[3]

In meeting her challenges, Isabel had the advantages of youth, spunk, and a husband who was also a good comrade. As a bride without children, she was free to ride and explore the countryside in a spirit of adventure and appreciation for the magnificent scenery whenever opportunity arose. She and James worked together and good-naturedly exchanged tasks that they would normally have assigned to each other on the basis of gender roles. Each did whatever needed to be done. Thus, in her character and demeanor, Isabel in many ways personified the "new woman" who was coming on the scene in both the United States and England by the 1880s. The new woman was the beneficiary of expanding educational, occupational, and professional opportunities and greater prosperity in both countries (although the opening of higher education for women lagged in England, as compared to America). The new woman was also blessed by a subtle cultural shift—underway for some time—in which marriage among the middle and upper classes had become more a companionate relationship based on mutual negotiation than one in which the husband ruled as dictator within the household.[4]

Being a lady, nonetheless, was somewhat different in each country. In the United States a lady was usually middle class, had fewer servants, and could expect to perform more physical labor than her English counterpart. The English lady, by contrast, usually came from a more elite class and was more likely to be a household manager overseeing a bevy of servants. Isabel expressed her English ideals when she noted, rather sarcastically, that all the women in surrounding families, including the one who sold her butter, were called *ladies.* Still, the prevailing views of proper family life and women's roles at home and in society—based on slightly different versions of the lady— were strikingly similar on the two sides of the Atlantic.[5]

Despite these commonalities, any Englishwoman who settled for any length of time in the United States auto- matically faced problems—chiefly, prejudice. England was the former mother country, and if upper-class Americans often sought to emulate the British, many others, especially those of Irish background, hated them. "Twisting the [British] Lion's tale," or saber rattling against England, was a popular political strategy politicians often used to win votes.[6] British travelers, sojourners, or settlers in America could handle this bias only by cultivating a thick skin. Unfortunately, many of them responded by asserting their supremacy in terms of cultural background and standards of propriety. Certainly the reader can discern an attitude of superiority in many of the letters Isabel wrote and later published.

For example, Isabel noted, with a tone of amusement, that in America servants were always referred to as "help" and not as servants. Initially Isabel employed the Morrises, a married couple whom she looked down on because they came from a poor section of London. She found them so lacking in cleanliness and competence that, before long, she terminated their employment. She refused, however, to hire American "help," since they were too "independent" and poorly trained. Violating her own English standards of ladylike behavior, she did her own housework and cooking. One can admire her resourcefulness, but she missed an important point. To Americans, the "help" were not part of a serving class as they were in England. Instead, according to the prevailing American dream of success, every citizen, of whatever occupation or station, was potentially a success story. One's hired "help" today was tomorrow's mistress of a prosperous farm or ranch or successful businessman or even the rising politician of tomorrow.[7] And while many Americans never overcame poverty and most who rose in status achieved only incremental improvement, mobility in America was greater than elsewhere and was a source of national pride.[8] After all, had not Andrew Carnegie started off as a poor immigrant boy from Scotland before becoming America's foremost industrialist?

Finally, Isabel made a grave and egregious mistake when she failed to edit her characterization of Americans as *natives* in her volume. There were several reasons why her former neighbors would be insulted. Chiefly, Americans had used the term *native* in their ethnocentric references to American Indians. With the Indian Wars almost over, most Native peoples were now on reservations, where many westerners, eager for their land, believed they belonged. Moreover, these same westerners had often justified Indian removal by adopting an ideology that saw American Indians as inferior to non-Indians. Even ethnologists of this era often viewed American Indians as people who were, on the evolutionary scale, more "childlike" than the rest of the American population and whose culture was "backward" and inferior to the culture of the United States as a whole.[9] Americans also knew that the British had created for themselves an empire "on which the sun never set," one based on dominion over people of color in Asia and Africa. The British often referred to these peoples as *natives* as well. Hence, as citizens in a country that had once been England's colony, Americans were sensitive to being characterized as *natives,* especially by one of Queen Victoria's subjects.

Richard Saunders tells us that Isabel probably imagined that her volume, published only with her initials and with names disguised, would not make its way into the hands of her former neighbors. It did, of course. The young woman, who had hoped to appeal to a British audience as widely and successfully as Isabella Bird had done with her volumes describing her travels in America, faced a different outcome. Isabel Randall became a pariah in the land where she and James had hoped to establish a successful Montana enterprise and an American dynasty as well. The bitter and freezing winter of 1886–87, which brought huge losses to ranchers on the Great Plains and in the Northwest and contributed to the eventual bankruptcy of the Moreland Ranch Stock Company, ended the Randalls' hopes for finding prosperity in Montana's Gallatin Valley.

But there is much more to Isabel Randall's volume than her family's business failure and the animosity she incurred from her former neighbors. Despite later events, Isabel's correspondence demonstrates that although many consider the trans-Mississippi West a place where men proved themselves by risking life and limb in a dangerous environment and unforgiving climate, women also met and passed their own personal tests of courage and stamina. Though one suspects that Isabel edited her letters to reflect her idealized version of herself—as most do in similar circumstances—enough honesty comes through to let us know that, most of the time, she proved herself a trooper. The West was not simply a place to start over and attain land and extract riches from the land, but a region where individuals were required to meet extraordinary challenges. When they did so with courage and a modicum of equanimity, they emerged with heightened self-respect. Writing in 1885, for example, Elizabeth Bacon Custer, the wife of the late Lieutenant Colonel George Armstrong Custer, noted that in the West she had experienced intense fear more than once. "When a woman has come out of danger, she is too utterly a coward by nature not to dread enduring the same thing again," she noted in *"Boots and Saddles,"* her memoir of army life in Dakota Territory in the 1870s. "But," she added, "it is something to know that she is equal to it." In the future, whatever dread or anxiety a woman felt, having mastered that fear, "she can count on rising to the situation when the hour actually comes."[10] As a young, intrepid Englishwoman, Isabel Randall overcame her fears and anxieties with courage, good judgment, and practicality.

Finally, in this volume, Isabel bequeathed valuable social history to the modern reader. Through Randall's letters, the reader learns about the stoves of the 1880s and how one made and kept household fires for heating and cooking. She discusses such matters as the driving of wild horses and why it was necessary to heat frozen bridles in wintertime to spare the horses' mouths and flesh. The reader discovers something about raising chickens and pigs in Montana, the irrigating that was necessary for gardens, and how families dealt with sleeping in bedrooms where the indoor temperature in winter sometimes registered zero. Summers, by contrast, were lovely with green prairies lush with wildflowers. However, they brought mosquitoes and the danger of rattlesnakes, especially when one was traveling or camping out.

Overall, Randall's volume provides a journey into the past, guided by a vivacious and sprightly heroine. Surely modern-day readers can forgive her for being careless in her terminology and something of a snob. She was supercilious at times, but all the more honest since this was who she really was—that and, in her best moments, a charming and enthusiastic observer who had a knack for writing vividly about everyday life in a West that is largely gone. Richard Saunders's expertly edited and annotated edition of Isabel F. Randall's *A Lady's Ranche Life in Montana* allows readers to recapture, with a sense of immediacy and freshness, life in southwestern Montana in the mid-1880s. Isabel Randall's West may have been challenging and, at times, difficult. However, it was not the proverbial "hell on horses and women" for her. When she stated that she was happier in Montana than she had been elsewhere, the reader should take her at her word. With her husband's companionship and that of his brother as well, with access to new books and her beloved piano and freedom to ride and explore, she found a life of "happiness" and "health," one that freed her from keeping up appearances. It says much about Isabel Randall that these were the priorities she valued most.

SHIRLEY A. LECKIE

Acknowledgments

Though this book is intensely local, the research for this edition has ranged far and wide. Serendipity has enriched the commentary and notes occasionally, generosity almost constantly. I offer my thanks to those who were either enormously helpful in their own right or simply had the right snippet of data at the right time, specifically, Chris and Ila Saunders, who put me up and put up with me; William Torrens, Local Studies Librarian of the Buckinghamshire County Council Education Office—one rarely finds a more cheerfully helpful professional; the Ordnance Survey people, who put together a terrific on-line search engine for British maps and place-names; John F. M. Dagger and his helpful associate, whose research filled in bare spots I could not otherwise patch; John C. Carlson and others from the Montana Natural Heritage Program, for many tentative flora and fauna identifications; Alice Blackford of the Oxford University Archives for help with university records; Ann Butterfield, Assistant Director for the Gallatin

Historical Society and Pioneer Museum; the Honorable John E. Greenall, Joint-Master of the Meynell and South Staffordshire Hunt; Lory Morrow, photo curator at the Montana Historical Society; Scott Christensen; Greg Notess; Kim Allen Scott; many lending libraries; and my clan, who unwittingly donated many evenings to this work and who make life in general worthwhile.

A Lady's Ranch Life
in Montana

Introduction
A British Settler in Context

For the English, the genre of the personal travel narrative has attracted and held readers since medieval times. Pilgrims like Sir John Mandeville began reporting their adventures to eager eleventh- and twelfth-century readers, and curiosity never flagged. No matter how much was available, there was always interest in more. But by the nineteenth century, the world was pretty well known. After seven hundred years, the surface of the globe was papered with thousands of descriptive works ranging between the Arctic and the Antarctic, from vineyards of the French countryside to the taro fields of South Sea islands, from the sky-scratching Nepalese Himalayas to the smoking highlands of Tierra del Fuego. Landscapes were becoming distinctly less interesting to readers than firsthand accounts of the peoples who populated them.

English Comments on the American West

Isabel FitzHerbert Randall's 1887 book of letters stands as one slim, hardly noticed item among scores of similar descriptive works written by European visitors commenting specifically on American life. Mrs. Randall's slender book describing life in Montana was a latecomer to the genre. She had been a married wife only a few days before departing the English countryside in the fall of 1884. A month later she settled eagerly into a log house in south-western Montana's Gallatin Valley, a few miles from the source of the Missouri River. Hers was not a migration, seeking better living conditions. Her move was an investment. Isabel's family background was one of gentility and privilege. She and her husband, James L. Randall, were there to participate in the last great American economic boom of the nineteenth century. Had their luck turned out differently, Isabel Randall might have become the matriarch of a Montana dynasty and remained unknown to history. Things did not work out; but regardless, she was eager to tell family and others back in Britain of her adventure on a Rocky Mountain horse ranch. The North American interior may have been a subject less titillating for English readers than it had been even fifty years earlier—the novelty of the Americas had waned somewhat—but reading material was still consumed in huge quantities in England during the Gilded Age, and there was always a market for something new and unique. To radically proper Victorian Britons, the wide-open social life of the American West was ever unique.

The contradictions in American social manners fascinated the nineteenth-century English. Daniel Boorstein, commenting on the published letters of one noted English traveller, Isabella Bird, commented that in western America the traveler was presented with "a world of vigilance committees, lynchings, and desperados quick on the trigger, who would shoot a friend for an 'impertinent remark.'" At the same time, Bird carefully noted that there were "few flagrant breaches of morality." Both life and property, she observed, were generally safer in wild Colorado than in urbane England. Boorstein points out that in her travels Isabella Bird reported "a brutish sullenness in public places and a shocking crudity of table manners; yet nowhere did she fail to find gentleness or chivalry. She found an oppressive lack of privacy among the exhilarating solitudes of the wild mountains. She found people pinchpenny, parsimonious, greedy, yet willing to share their short rations or escort her on horseback hundreds of miles through a snowstorm."[1] This was Excitement, this was Real Life, and the English loved it. She was not alone. Robert Athern cataloged 140 published expatriate narratives, diaries, and books of collected letters contemporary with Randall's work. The English often came from urbane Britannia to the American frontier in a quest for firsthand experience with the "real," the Wild West. What genteel travelers generally found upon arrival were bad accommodations and a disquieting social democracy; what they ruefully discovered after a bit of local experience was that they were chasing shadows and ideals. Even as they arrived eager and expectant in dusty cow towns and gritty mining camps, the log-cabin frontier was being quickly papered and lace curtained into gentility by progressive local boosters. It was not only sightseers like Bird who came west, however. Fortune seekers and investors flocked to western farming and stock-raising opportunities. They tended to write less frequently about their experiences than English travelers, since they came not to report but to profit. Their perspectives as on-the-ground participants makes their rarer observations the more interesting and important.

Isabella Bird's descriptive letters were first presented to the English in 1878, published serially in the magazine *Leisure Hour.* Collected almost immediately into book form, by 1882 the letters were circulating in their seventh British edition and had an envious reputation; the book had been translated into French and seen several American editions as well. Bird's work remains one of the great first-hand descriptions of the late American frontier. Isabella Bird titled her enormously popular letters *A Lady's Life in the Rocky Mountains.*

A few years later, Isabel Randall gave her own book of letters the title *A Lady's Ranche Life in Montana,* and her choice may have been no coincidence.[2] The striking similarity between the titles suggests that Isabel Randall was well aware of Bird's notable work and may have been hoping that her own book would be similarly received. It was not. Randall's book seems to have been generally overlooked in England and the rest of America, but it is wry understatement to say that *A Lady's Ranche Life in Montana* was merely "noticed" in Montana. The few surviving perceptions suggest that Isabel's Moreland neighbors were downright indignant over the work. But introducing that tale gets ahead of the story. Those factual bits are related in the epilogue. At this point it is important to note that in Isabel Randall's book we have one of a very few works for which there is record of the American response to the published work of a foreign traveler—Isabel left us her opinion, and we have her neighbors' opinions of her opinion.

Despite sharp criticism of what she saw in the West, Isabella Bird's longer, more detailed book was popular with English readers because of her ability to perceive and illustrate character beyond immediate circumstance, making Bird a paragon window into the time and the people she saw. The lack of that redeeming quality made Isabel Randall more typical of her self-absorbed social class at the time and of British colonial mentality. It is ironic that through her work we know an English expatriate better than we do the people she sought to portray. Though her critiques of American culture were typical of British writers of the period, her comments bit more deeply because unlike Bird, Isabel Randall was tied to a specific community. Isabel's inability to see far beyond class and propriety doomed her socially in Montana and proved the essential truth of Coleridge's quip that "The best people in the mother country will generally be the worst in the colonies."[3] Isabel's morals did not decline; rather, her upbringing conditioned her perception of the new world in which she found herself, and she paid the price for her prejudice.

Part of Isabel's trouble may have stemmed from mis-understanding the role of correspondent. Isabella Bird's letters home were written specifically for publication; Isabel Randall's letters were a *private* correspondence, not written for wider readership at all. To be fair, the women were about equally subjective, but due to their differing purposes the two women's writings were nonequivalent. Isabella Bird's book represents the West from the detached view-point of a traveler and socially distant observer. Conversely, Isabel Randall's letters are valuable to modern readers because they are a firsthand record by a social participant, although today one might uncharitably regard her as "clueless." She provides insights into personal activities and daily routine that are very scarce in contemporary records. Notice, for instance, that in Isabel's world the men of her household not only shared the burden of domestic chores, but she praises them for their demonstrated abilities. Isabel fully expected to reciprocate shared labor as well, participating occasionally with the livestock beyond caring for the farmyard (chickens, pigs, and her ample garden). The frontier chauvinism Dee Garceau describes did not seem to taint the Randall household.[4] Gender boundaries to her work world did exist, however. While Isabel assumed responsibility for part of the farm chores, she did *not* participate in exchanging labor with other ranch women as men typically did (characterized by the roundup she describes), just as most other men did not share in the domestic economies she occasionally mentions when visiting other households.

Despite her genteel upbringing and to her credit, Isabel learned much from her Montana stay. Most of that education fell within the realm of "domestic science"—six months into her adventure, rather than relying on servants, the mistress of the house was doing her own cooking and cleaning and commenting to her incredulous family how *fulfilling* such activity was. Pointedly, however, she does not record that she had stooped to laundry (as an uncharitable critic later mentions sidelong), but she may not have wanted to admit that—laundering actually was servile, about the lowest occupational level at which a woman could maintain a shred of self-respect in the eyes of polite English society.

As primary source material, Randall's book supports the perspectives of widely differing interpretive theses, reminding us that there is no *single* "western experience" to be generalized for gender, ethnicity, class, or locale.

Frederick Jackson Turner and his students defined western American history by claiming that the American frontier shaped individuals and European society into a different, more democratic, and distinctly American culture. Isabel Randall may have originated in and considered herself in a class above her neighbors, but she also came to *do* the things they did on a daily basis: tending to domestic stock, cultivating a vegetable garden, and housework—hardly traditional occupations of a leisured gentlewoman. Her daily life was definitely conducted on the same footing as that of her neighbors. Conversely, Patricia Limerick and proponents of the New Western History redefined the scholarly approach to the larger region by contending that emigrants hauled along and sought to reproduce the cultures that they had known, wherever they moved.[5] If Mrs. Randall demanded higher standards than her neighbors for the results of domestic labor, well, she had come from a milieu in which such services were typically performed by full-time professionals. While Isabel and her household rig a lawn-tennis court, as they feed themselves upon "puddings," occupying themselves with fishing and shooting, they are reproducing the lives and pastimes they led and occupied in merry old England. Nevertheless, Isabel Randall's letters reveal the pride she felt in her accomplishments and even the pleasure she learned to take in domestic routine. Part of the motivation for compiling and editing her letters probably stems from this process of a woman's discovery of herself as a skilled individual. As a microcosm of the frontier experience, Isabel Randall's letters confirm elements of both Turner's and Limerick's generalized interpretations.

Isabel's edited letters and the reaction to them also illustrate other major points made by scholars. First, as Randall notes in her own preface, the book is presented to readers in terms that emphasize the positive qualities defining the "Progressive Era" in U.S. history—success, achievement, optimism, and economic development— and as such confirms Elizabeth Hampsten's observations about women's private writings being a "literature of omission."[6] Second, the book illustrates the fact that there was no single, definable uniformity to the female experience on the American frontier. Work and privilege shaped social interaction and life experience, even if "class" was particularly disdained as an American reality. The relative economic stability Randall enjoyed allowed her to transcend the type of ceaseless labor and grinding poverty that characterized the life of Emily French, a contemporary Colorado diarist. Neither was Isabel's life the ceaseless cycle of hard work noted by Nannie Alderson or Evelyn Cameron, or the success and wealth that Mrs. Nat Collins found in the stock industry.[7] Third, the letters show that Americans flatly did not appreciate the publication of unvarnished foreign opinions about their world, particularly opinions that questioned the practical results of their progressive ideals, no matter how accurate or descriptive they might be.[8] Unfortunately, the descriptions and impressions that most interested English readers were what Americans least wanted to have said of them. Isabel's private observations on the world she inhabited were precisely what offended her contemporary neighbors. Even after being stewed in the frontier's egalitarian "melting pot," it seems that Americans still found the English hard to swallow.

Isabel Randall's World

Isabel Randall (née FitzHerbert) belonged to one shoot of a well-established English family. William, son of Herbert (therefore "fitz-Herbert") was granted Norbury Manor in 1125, barely fifty years after the Norman Conquest. Roots of the large and scattered Fitzherbert family have remained in and around this corner of Derbyshire, at the southern foot of the Peak District in the English Midlands, ever since. As wealthy landowners, the family has constituted the local aristocracy for nearly eight hundred years. Isabel's ancestral branch of the Fitzherberts acquired an estate at Tissington, an ancient holding north of Ashborne, in the mid-sixteenth century. At about the same time, that branch of the family fell in with the Anglican division of the church and began spelling the surname with the patronym capitalized behind the particle. Those descending through the Tissington line thus became FitzHerberts; those who remained Catholic kept the traditional spelling of Fitzherbert.[9]

Some two hundred years later, William FitzHerbert, Isabel's paternal great-grandfather, was created baronet by King George III in 1784. Isabel's grandfather inherited the Tissington estate and the title at the untimely death of an older brother, but Isabel's father, John Knight FitzHerbert, was a fifth son with almost no hope to the title or legacy.[10] As the son of a baronet he could at least properly claim the nominally honorific title "Esquire," but it was with the privilege of school at Harrow and as a Cambridge University–educated lawyer and justice of the peace that John maintained his station as a respectable gentleman. In the class-crazed world of nineteenth-century England, these counted for much.[11]

John married at thirty-nine, relatively late in life. His bride, Arabella Penelope White, was a Dublin native and therefore Irish or perhaps Scots-Irish. After their marriage the couple settled in Hulland, a mile or two east of the small market town of Ashbourne, Derbyshire. Here the family was only a few miles south and east of the ancestral home at Tissington Hall. A little over a year later, towards the end of September 1860, John and Arabella's eldest child was born, a little girl whom they named Isabel.[12] A son, Henry, joined his sister in 1862, Maude came the year following, and Godfrey, another son, arrived in 1864. Before Rachell Helen came in 1868 and finally Edith arrived in 1874, the John FitzHerberts had relocated another dozen miles south and east to Breadsall, a village immediately north of Derby.[13]

John FitzHerbert left the Midlands for the southern English coast around 1877. The family settled into Holdenhurst, a small Hampshire village five miles east of the resort city of Bournemouth and about half that distance inland from the English Channel. Holdenhurst, near the confluence of the Rivers Stour and Moors, had been a crossroads of significance for several hundred years. Today it is little more than an outlying neighborhood that roars with the noise of jets on their final landing approach to Bournemouth International Airport and highway traffic along route A338 into the city. Most of the barns, outbuildings, and dwellings in this English village that were standing during the FitzHerberts' time are gone, though a few rows of neat stone houses and St. John's Church remain.

In Holdenhurst, John FitzHerbert served as justice of the peace, a position similar to county judge in the United

States. At this time the justice's functions included both civil and criminal jurisdictions. Still, in such a small community John would have enjoyed ample personal leisure time and sufficient opportunity in private law practice to maintain a well-regulated house. By the time the census taker arrived to enroll the family in 1881, only Isabel and her three younger sisters remained to be listed as children in the household; the two FitzHerbert boys had probably been sent away to school. The enumeration suggests that the family's finances were sufficiently secure to allow them the luxury of employing servants. The household included the family's Irish cook, a housemaid, and a domestic nurse, who was probably Edith's primary care-giver.[14] The family's position was such that they occupied a comfortable station in life and were accustomed to having servants do most of the less genteel work, such as washing and ironing, and the endless cleaning required in a house that burned several coal grates for warmth. The household may have done their own gardening, in which most members would have taken turn, or relied upon the services of a hired gardener. By this time Isabel was a maiden of twenty.

In the late 1800s England stood at the world's economic apex. Britain had profited enormously in the Industrial Revolution, despite the emigration of tens of thousands of skilled and unskilled laborers to colonial holdings and North America. Its influence—colonial and economic—spanned the globe to such an extent that it could be said "the sun never sets upon the Empire." Science, industry, and capital combined to wring profit from the earth's peoples and natural resources. This was the day when the great trusts and corporations of the early twentieth century were in their infancy. There were tremendous fortunes to be made abroad, not only in England's colonies, but in the other enterprising markets around the world. For the investor, opportunity could knock repeatedly, competition was fierce, and prizes were won by the energetic, the ruthless, or the lucky. It was a heady time to be a young man of means looking for opportunity.

On the other hand, only one option for raising social or economic status remained open to a young Englishwoman, particularly for one of the lower and middle classes—to marry up. Yes, an adventuress could flout convention to win a reputation on her own, but the few who did so usually succeeded only by relying upon the stability of family connections, inherited money, or brash derring-do. Isabel FitzHerbert took the traditional route. Some time early in the 1880s, while she was in her twenties or per-haps in her late teens, she met a young gentleman with whom she soon established a relationship. In the unfor-tunate position of third son, James L. Randall had neither nobility nor family position to his credit. But no matter, he had a suitable family background, was well educated, and had ties to America that suggested—no, they promised—the possibility of a dramatic leap in his fortunes. She eventually accepted his suit and proposal of marriage, and in September 1884, perhaps at St. John's in Holdenhurst, Isabel assumed her husband's surname of Randall. About their courtship we can surmise only one fact—that a good portion of it was conducted from halfway around the world.

James Lowndes Randall, Isabel's husband, was born toward the end of March 1855 at or near Graffham, in Sussex, forty-five miles south and west of London. About his mother, Wilhelmina, we have only a given name and place of birth, St. Petersburg, Russia. Richard William Randall, James's father, had prepared for a career in the ministry at Oxford (Christ Church College, 1842; M.A. 1849; a D.D. would come in 1892) and was an Anglican high churchman. He was positioned as rector of Lavington, a Sussex parish, when his third son was born.[15]

Long before James Randall and Isabel FitzHerbert were introduced, family connections had smoothed his admission to Oxford University. At a time when collegiate education was primarily a study of classics, philosophy, history, and theology, James L. Randall carried to Montana's rough-edged valleys not only an Oxford University degree (New Inn Hall, 1876) but a master's degree as well (1879). James's education suggests that he had either planned to follow in the family business as an English high-church cleric or trained for the bar. Other Randall brothers also attended Oxford, though none attained to the degrees their older brother held. Besides two younger brothers, Cyril Wilberforce and Francis Henry, James had a sister, Mary, three years older than himself, and two sisters younger than Francis.[16] In 1881 Wilhelmina was twenty, Isabel's age, and Geraldine was a scholar of eighteen. As rector of the parish, Richard William Randall occupied a community position that required a suitable complement of domestic staff. The house thus maintained and included three female servants besides the family cook and Geraldine's governess.[17]

Membership among the country's gentry provided James Randall the means and chance to pursue opportunities when they were presented. Despite his education, he must have possessed a native restlessness, or perhaps the lure of riches was too great. Between 1881 and 1883 he abandoned what progress he had made toward law or a churchly career and determined to seek his fortune abroad in the United States. After an eventful year the foundation was laid; James returned to England in the late summer of 1884 to claim his bride. He and Isabel married a few weeks or days after his return and left for the North American interior almost immediately after their marriage. James had staked his fortunes in Montana Territory on the western American livestock boom and there was no time to lose.

The great period of English emigration to the United States had ended in the 1850s, thirty years earlier. A larger flood of immigrants from continental Europe now poured hungrily into American cities. Thanks to steam-driven transport and early developments in refrigeration, Europeans at home were developing a taste for imported American beef. To feed them all required enormous production and distribution markets. Sitting at the nexus of a railroad network, Chicago was well on its way to becoming the City of the Big Shoulders, a clearinghouse and processing center for agricultural products generated by the newly established and rapidly expanding farms and ranches of the trans-Mississippi West. The new opportunities caught the attention of Englishmen, attracting not only travelers and sightseers. Hundreds invested their youth and fortunes to chase opportunity far onto the arid plains of New Mexico, Colorado, Wyoming, and Montana.[18]

Despite the fears later expressed by Isabel's friends and relations, Montana—and the Gallatin Valley specifically—was hardly a howling wilderness. The West's last mining boom in the Black Hills was over. The Union Pacific Railroad had linked the California coast to the rest of the country twelve years earlier, and other transcontinental lines were threading westward. By the early 1880s Montana's Native residents were being conveniently pushed onto reservations by the U.S. military, farming was turning fertile mountain valleys under the plough, and the range cattle industry was already well established and poised to boom. Montana Territory already was. Investment capital from the United States and abroad was pouring into the region, financing ventures in timber harvesting in the west, mineral ventures in the central part of the territory, and livestock raising across central and eastern Montana.

During the first half of the 1880s, the free-range stock industry boomed the way that Montana's gold, then silver, and finally copper mines had boomed through the preceding twenty-five years. Montana had been carved out of Idaho Territory in the wake of the placer gold boom of 1864. Millions of dollars of granular treasure were washed out of the mountain gravels in places like Bannack, Grasshopper, and Alder gulches even while attention shifted to quartz mining and silver and the riches to be made there and finally to the rich copper ores around Butte.

At the same time to the south and east, on the high, wind-washed plains, wanton destruction of buffalo herds fed transcontinental railroad crews through the 1860s and '70s. The extermination of the buffalo vacated the ecological niche held by the major vegetative harvester on the plains. This allowed several years of an unnaturally rich forage crop to luxuriantly carpet the landscape. By 1880 the central and eastern Montana landscape was a rich, unbounded sea of highly nutritive grasses—bunch grass, buffalo grass, bluestem, gramma, and others—that had fed millions of grazing animals for untold years. That profusion of uncropped grass set the stage for Montana's second great boom, in livestock.

The natural landscape literally provided fodder for the western livestock boom, but the stock industry explosion of the 1880s was possible primarily because of U.S. land law. Montana was a U.S. territory. Under the terms of a grant of territorial status, all land that had not been previously claimed or offered for public sale became federal property and was thereafter not subject to further "private entry" or unregistered ownership claim. Creation as a federal territory in 1864 put Montana's seemingly limitless landscape directly under federal control, to be distributed piecemeal under federal law specifically to miners and homesteaders. But mines occupied only small parcels of land compared to farming, and for twenty years there seemed to be little public interest in settling and farming either the high plains or isolated mountain valleys. Therefore, most land in Montana was sitting not only unused but also *unclaimed*. "In this vast free pasturage," said a writer in a description of central Montana, "no one need really own an acre of land and thus far few have cared to." Until the land was actually deeded over to someone, the grass was simply there for the taking. The use of unclaimed public land for grazing, the writer also noted, "gives stock men free use of ranges, exempt from taxation of the lands." Could it get any better? Not only did you not have to own what your stock grazed, you did not have to pay taxes on it either. As long as grass grew across large stretches of the Montana landscape, every promoter noted that there were fortunes—big ones—to be made in Montana livestock.[19] "Cotton was once crowned king," crowed one eastern livestock journal, "but grass is now. . . . [and]

If grass is King, the Rocky Mountain region is its throne and fortunate indeed are those who possess it." That was the incredible promise of the free-range livestock boom—one did not have to *own,* or *maintain,* or *account for* the land to possess its riches. Livestock *would* multiply and mature on the plains, it was merely an issue of who would be on hand to reap the profits. Wealth itself could be conducted as a simple extractive industry. Isabel Randall's letters virtually breathe the excitement of the time.

Of all the opportunities Montana offered speculators of the 1880s, livestock required the least investment. One could get in with a few thousand dollars, an adventurous soul or two willing to run the operation, and a branding iron. Reports of 20 percent returns on cattle ventures, 30 percent on sheep, and as high as 40 percent profits on horses were commonplace. "The average profit realized can without any doubt be placed at two per cent. per month on all capital invested in cattle in Montana," wrote one promoter.[20] "Some of the wealthiest farmers in the county were known by the writer when they had not fifty dollars to call their own," said another. If genuine wealth could really be made on that scale, then the potential return on *substantial* capital investment overwhelmed imagination. Money cascaded in accordingly.

Free resources and available capital, however, were only two considerations in fueling the livestock boom—there were other contributing factors as well. Transportation, or the ability to move people and goods in and out of a given location, is the major issue in any development. With watercourse navigation severely limited by the West's geography, railroad access became *the* determining factor in land development and western economic growth during the late nineteenth century. Though herds from Montana ranches began trailing to markets as early as the mid-1860s, the railroad bestowed upon the rancher the capability to ship his stock directly to urban markets in the East without losing pounds from trail wear. When work on the Northern Pacific Rail Road promised a tangible link between Washington's fisheries and timber resources and the rest of the country, promoters began touting the stock-raising benefits of Montana's high plains. The railroad neared completion in 1883, just as interest in Montana stock raising peaked—spoon-fed by the railroad itself, of course.

As in any boom, those who were in first stood to make the most. The psychology of opportunity—created and fueled by the interests of railroad and then local promoters—made the most of the moment. The burning interest in the livestock scheme created a ready market for promotional newspaper stories, books, booklets, and guides of various sorts. Even communities bid for a piece of the action. Matt W. Alderson's small booklet *Bozeman: A Guide to Its Places of Recreation and a Synopsis of Its Superior Natural Advantages, Industries, and Opportunities,* for instance, advertised the agricultural advantages of the Gallatin Valley specifically.[21] By far the most influential work was James S. Brisbin's *The Beef Bonanza; or, How to Get Rich on the Plains,* a book widely credited with creating the European rush to the West. James Randall almost certainly saw and read this work, and probably also fellow Englishman W. Baillie Grohman's descriptive article "Cattle Ranches in the Far West." Brisbin was an army officer with experience across the central and northern West and had commanded Fort Ellis, a post in the Gallatin Valley a few miles east of Bozeman, from 1877 to 1879. He had experienced all the geographic and climatic rigors the region offered, yet despite this could report virtually nothing negative of the West or of its opportunities for stock raising. In his book Colonel Brisbin cited and featured the figures for horse ranching in the Gallatin Valley specifically.[22] There is no actual record of what persuaded James Randall to come to the United States, and to Montana in particular, but he was a gentleman with a taste for the life of a sportsman. Cattle would not have attracted him, but the culturally respectable position of horse breeder would have—and all available figures suggested that horse raising generated the most substantial return on an investment.

What an opportunity! Unimaginably huge tracts of open land, no taxes, ready markets, and growing demand—it was almost too good to be true. In fact it was, as the Randalls and other would-be ranchers discovered across the western plains. Behind the promotional façades lurked natural factors either missed entirely or conveniently ignored.

As in most boom cycles, the thirst for return on investment was constructed upon several unsound assumptions. First, that the steep growth curve characterizing the expansion of a new industry could be maintained over time. This is simply untrue. Those who get in first make money, usually by selling out to those who come later hoping to "ride the wave" to fortune. Latecomers shoulder the costs of the downturn—venture failures and consolidation, the "bust" as the market stabilizes—that inevitably follows a boom.

Second, environmental assumptions proved false, namely, that one grazing animal was like any other, and that since the plains had fed millions of buffalo it could similarly feed millions of beef cattle, sheep, and horses without serious consideration of differences between the animals.[23] Reality was a little more problematic. The grass may have been nutritious, but buffalo are a good deal hardier than domestic livestock. During the first half of the decade (including the 1885–86 season, which Isabel Randall was on hand to record), several years of abnormally mild winter conditions gave Montana's new arrivals a false impression of the high-plains climate. Boom ranchers had no experience with the way that subzero temperatures, driven knifelike into the gut by an icy wind, would cut down a herd or rider on the unprotected plains. The bitter winter of 1886–87 was on the scale of a natural disaster, and it crippled the free-range stock boom not just in Montana, but across the West from Texas to Canada. This was the year that a skinny cowpuncher named Charles M. Russell responded to his boss's inquiry about the status of the wintering herd by sketching out the famous "Waiting for a Chinook" or "The Last of 5,000" drawings, showing a single lean cow standing in a snowbank, fending off wolves. Nobody factored capricious high-plains weather or its severity into promotional tales.

The rush into large-scale livestock raising crowded the few sheltered ecosystems that were unnaturally rich from the temporary absence of grazers. For instance, Brisbin reported that Gallatin County grazed 30,333 head of cattle and 8,033 horses in 1879. By 1887 Gallatin County alone was grazing 10,673 horses, 16,421 cattle, and 13,220 sheep—over 40,000 animals, exclusive of native wildlife, concentrated in the Gallatin Valley and its northern rim of surrounding hills.[24] Across the plains, competing ranch operations quickly overpopulated the desirable range locations, leaving marginal land for the latecomers. Their products flooded the beef market, forcing down prices. In addition, those from outside the region generally seem to have underestimated the investment of manpower and constant effort needed to work stock. The grass may have been there for the taking, but it required vigor, stamina, and plain hard work to maintain free-ranging livestock on the nearly limitless face of this grassy ocean.

Finally, land claims and the fences wielded by growing numbers of settlers after 1885 threatened the maintenance of open ranges. U.S. land policy, a direct result of the Northwest Ordinances passed a century earlier, had been enacted to encourage small-parcel settlement and political organization. That policy failed utterly to comprehend the issues of either arid-land agriculture or ranching. Homestead policy that worked in the forested Midwest was entirely unsuitable for addressing the issues of the American West, but under its protection the landscape of the Great Plains was carved up into scattered smallholdings and towns surrounded by large open tracts of public land.

Propped up by a stream of investment capital and not by generated profits, the boom of the 1880s could not last. The free-range stock industry was naively founded on unrealistic expectations, force-fed a potent combination of weather and naiveté, crippled by the inability to control the unbounded public land it needed but never owned, and finally forced to scale back and operate on a more realistic (and sustainable) basis by the market it supplied but could never dominate.[25]

But for the moment it did not matter—Montana was riding the bubble. In the 1880 census Bozeman was a village of merely 894 souls. Ten years later the town had grown threefold to 2,143 residents. The county population had grown as well if not quite as steeply.[26] By 1882 track-laying crews of the Northern Pacific were within months of completing that transcontinental rail line and halted in their westward drive only long enough to lay a fifty-mile spur down the Paradise Valley to Cinnabar, positioning the railroad to open the way for Yellowstone Park tourism on a grand scale. The rails crested Bozeman Pass in the closing months of 1882 and arrived in Bozeman the following March.[27] By the first week of April 1883, the rails already stretched fifteen miles west of Bozeman and were being laid at the rate of nearly a mile a day.[28] English entrepreneur James L. Randall arrived several weeks later.[29] With him were his younger brother Frank and a cousin, Harry Lowndes.

By blind chance or by prior arrangement, the trio of Englishmen fell in with Alexander H. Beattie, William E. Cullen, and William D. Flowers. Cullen and Beattie were officers of the territorial district court and were then in Bozeman attending to court business. Outside the courtroom the pair pursued small-time capital ventures in the territory, like virtually everyone else. One of these prospects was to buy heavily in property around Hamilton, a townsite near the center of the Gallatin Valley, expecting the town to grow and land prices to increase with the railroad's arrival.[30] Unfortunately the railroad surveyors passed a couple of miles north of Hamilton without slowing down or even glancing in their direction, making property in the struggling town distinctly less valuable. Rather than abandon plans, the foundationless wood-frame buildings were simply hitched to teams and skidded to a new place beside the tracks.[31] Residents and promoters expected to keep the same name after the town was repositioned, but

Ravalli County's larger community won out with the U.S. Post Office, so Gallatin's "new" community was renamed Moreland.

Discussion among the members of the Randall group and Flowers, Cullen, and Beattie resulted in an informal agreement to pool resources and form a corporation, the Moreland Ranch Stock Company (MRSC). James Randall was appointed, elected, or claimed the privilege of acting as trustee and assumed the practical management of the firm's stock business. He evidently brought with him the equivalent of several thousand dollars in pounds sterling to establish himself. Acting as trustee on October 22, 1883, Randall signed a contract purchasing land from the Northern Pacific's federal land subsidy. Within days a second contract was signed as well, pushing the total purchase to over 3,200 acres.[32]

Several months later in March 1884, the stockholders of the Moreland Ranch Stock Company incorporated with a capital limit of $300,000 for a term of twenty years over the signatures of future Montana governor Wilber F. Sanders, William D. Flowers, James Lowndes Randall, Alexander H. Beattie, Henry G. Walsh, Henry L. Lowndes, Frank (Francis Henry) Randall, and William E. Cullen. Flowers was president, Cullen vice president, and Sanders functioned as secretary. The terms of incorporation were written to include everything that the partners were already doing and about as broadly as language could express other business purposes. The MRSC was established:

> For the purpose of breeding, raising, buying, and selling Live Stock of all kinds; raising, buying, and selling grain, hay, vegetables, and Generally all kinds of Farm produce;

selling water for irrigating purposes, or for purposes of power for mills or machinery, milling and manufacturing flour, lumber and other products; general merchandising; buying, selling, renting, leasing and generally dealing in real estate.[33]

Besides the three English newcomers, each of the stockholders already had a stake established in or around Moreland. In effect, Moreland's businessmen and investors were banding together. Randall's purchases were thus intended less as a basis specifically for a stock-raising concern—which could be done at no cost on the unfenced lands all around them—but for capitalizing on the town's agricultural and developmental potential and squeezing profits from general agricultural commodity prices. This diversification distributed capital risk and put the firm into the position of profiting from the local boom in newly opened agricultural production. Land ownership, which stock-raising promoters generally dismissed, positioned the company to control (and profit by) growth in the area immediately around Moreland.

Throughout May 1884, James Randall signed deeds adding half a dozen more parcels of privately owned land to the MRSC's holdings, mostly properties belonging to the firm's stockholders. By June the combination owned outright almost seven thousand acres.[34] It controlled all land surrounding the Moreland town site on three sides. Even in undeveloped land it was a tremendous holding for one man, and larger than many of Britain's country estates. The partners probably realized that as well, and on May 15 Randall filed a trust declaration in Bozeman that bound him to hold the property he had acquired "only for

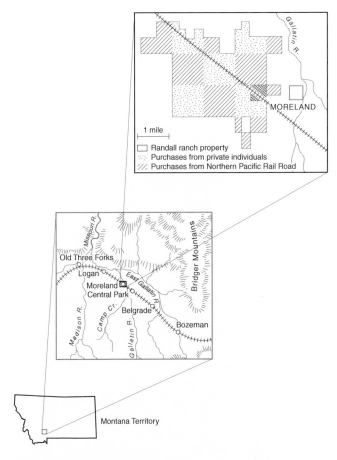

Randall ranch and vicinity, Montana Territory. Cartography
by AthertonCustoms, 2003.

the use benefit and behalf of the Stockholders of the Moreland Ranch Stock Company (Limited)."[35]

Parcels of land owned by various stockholders but *not* deeded to the MRSC increased the total acreage the firm nominally controlled. James made time to locate one place for himself, not subject to the firm's cooperative ownership. This well-watered quarter section of land, 160 acres, sat about a mile directly east of Moreland. The property was bisected by a low bluff. The western half was on the dry valley floor, while the eastern half dipped down to the gravelly beds and willow-choked coulees of the Gallatin river bottoms. The original property claim had been made in the 1860s by simply planting a stake in the middle of the shallow stream and describing a territorial claim from that point. At the base of the bluff, out of the wind, the owner had constructed a rough but roomy cabin. About 1870 the cabin was enlarged by a two-story, squared-log addition. Its double-hung windows and a glassed entry door with side lites of colored glass made it the grandest home in the valley at the time. A stone, barrel-vaulted dairy was constructed beside the original structure, in addition to a square horseshoe of barns, stables, and outbuildings on the bluff above.[36]

For a few years the house served as the Gallatin Valley Female Seminary, a girls' school. The school did not do well and had closed by 1875. By the late 1870s ownership changed again, and yet again in 1883. James Randall finally acquired the property and improvements in 1884. Though larger, grander homes had been constructed in Bozeman by this time, what has since been wrongly identified as the "Culver house" was probably the only structure in Moreland's immediate area suitable for the refined tastes of the girl James Randall intended to make his wife.[37]

Having established himself in Moreland, James was finally in a position to settle permanently and prepared to return to England to claim his bride. Travel was expensive. On May 8, James mortgaged his new property to an uncle in England, Buckingham Cathedral's archdeacon, James Leslie Randall, raising $2,400 to finance the trip to Britain and back. He arrived at Holdenhurst in late August and, if he had not proposed to Isabel earlier by letter, presented his suit. She accepted. James and Isabel were married during the first week of September 1884.[38] She was turning twenty-four, he was twenty-nine.

Departure preparations probably consumed their attentions for a month; the ocean voyage and rail trip to Montana would be their honeymoon tour. From Liverpool on or near the first of October 1884, the couple took ship as First Class Cabin passengers aboard the S.S. *Wisconsin,* bound for New York. Customs documents citing their arrival note only that they were disembarking "PS," or were making a "protracted sojourn."[39] From New York they took the train via Niagara Falls to Chicago, where they made a brief stay with friends and which Isabel summarized for her family in the first letter appearing in her later book. From Chicago, the Northern Pacific Rail Road took them on to St. Paul, and thence across the Dakota and Montana plains to the Gallatin Valley. The couple arrived in Moreland after the middle of October 1884.

Isabel's letters home to the family begin with her arrival in Moreland. As will be seen, Isabel relates the challenges of her life in the colder, drier, distinctly foreign environment of a Montana stock ranch with a mixture of delight, fascination, and optimism. For two and a half years, between October 1884 and July 1886, Isabel's letters home provided her parents and sisters in England a descriptive window into her faraway world.

Isabel's letters were edited for publication and presented to the reading public during an extended trip home to England during the winter of 1886–87. She thus missed the horrific winter that doomed the West's open-range stock industry and ultimately her own fortunes. Documentary records concerning her and James certainly survive in various places, but relatively little is presently known about the Randalls after the publication of her book. Isabel did return to Montana following its publication, most likely in the late spring or summer of 1887, and rejoined James in Moreland. What is known about that second two-year stay is related in the epilogue.

The James Randalls returned to England permanently in the winter of 1889 or early spring of 1890, essentially fleeing declining fortunes and staving off failure. The western livestock bubble had burst. Like so many others who leaped into the livestock boom, James and the Moreland Ranch Stock Company seem to have overestimated their opportunities and underestimated the investment of luck and labor needed for both ranching and agriculture in an arid environment. Isabel's letters hint at contributing factors to their failure: the shortage of suitable labor for such a large and diverse operation, possibly too much land under cultivation, crop and stock losses due to harsh winter weather and a summer drought, and bad luck. The Randalls themselves seem never to have adequately recovered from the disastrous barn fire Isabel relates in detail. While diversification of interests can be a protective move, the available human resources of the Moreland Ranch Stock Company—which seem to consist primarily of James and Frank Randall's unstinting labor—were divided too thinly among too many chores. The drought during the 1889 growing season probably capped their decision to leave. "Water is scarce in the streams of the valley and many wells of the city are said to be lower than during cold, wintry weather," noted one contemporary writer.[40] Since James seems to have contributed primarily his labor after the initial land purchases, he was evidently able to recoup his investment by selling out to his partners and walked away from the MRSC without incurring a major capital loss.

The couple expended five years of youth and effort on their Montana venture. Whatever anxiety they felt about leaving was certainly outweighed by a desire to escape the social consequences of Isabel's literary venture. By 1889 Isabel Randall's book had offended most or all of the small community in Moreland. Especially if they got away with their capital relatively intact, they must have welcomed the relief of leaving behind the animosity of their Moreland neighbors. Their relief was demonstrated in one other way as well. Having arrived home in England, by March of 1890 Isabel was expecting a baby. Her confinement came late in the fall while the couple was living again near Bournemouth. Basil FitzHerbert Randall, the couple's only child, was delivered on November 2.[41]

Even had they been planning or hoping to return some day to their western homestead, by the time of Basil's birth it was evident that nothing remained in Montana for the Randalls to return to. By 1890 the Moreland Ranch

Stock Company was essentially a shell, property rich but with a tenth of the ranch stock James had driven eastward in 1886. The following year the firm held only the value of its mortgaged land. In 1892 the Moreland Ranch Stock Company formally dissolved and its tax liability was cancelled.[42]

James and Isabel at last sold their Montana homestead to New York brewer Henry Altenbrand in December 1890. Altenbrand was busily buying up property and water rights around Moreland, laying the operational foundation for the Manhattan Malting Company. Starting with the property of the Moreland Ranch Stock Company and expanding outward, the Manhattan Malting Company eventually controlled three times as much property as the MRSC had, but it had investment backing to match and ready markets for the malted barley that it produced. As early as the end of 1890, Altenbrand and the MMC became the controlling interest in the Moreland area. William Flowers and R. Hugh Sawyer, both former stockholders in the Moreland Ranch Stock Company, signed a petition with Altenbrand to change the town's name from Moreland to Manhattan in 1891.[43] Until Prohibition killed the malting business in the 1920s, Manhattan was essentially an agricultural company town.

James and Isabel Randall are never known to have returned to Montana or to the United States. In 1892 Richard William Randall, James' father, retired from the deanship of Chichester Cathedral. Isabel's father, John K. FitzHerbert, passed away in 1894. Shortly thereafter James, Isabel, and Basil moved to Sudbury, Derbyshire, within Isabel's family's country. James's occupation was that of a country gentleman, which suggests that the family was

sufficiently well-off to require no occupation. He partici-
pated actively with the Meynell Hunt, riding to hounds
and hunting foxes across the hedges and hills. James
gained his own reputation as a writer in 1901 when, at
the request of club members, he wrote and published a
two-volume *History of the Meynell Hounds and Country,*
which became a classic work of English sporting literature
and remains a collectible book.[44]

Isabel's book never gained the notoriety that James's
did, but she took pleasures in other successes. Their son,
Basil, determined to follow a military career and was
commissioned as an Army lieutenant in 1911, the same
year that Manhattan, Montana, incorporated. Basil was
appointed to the Indian Cavalry and posted to Baluchistan
(today western Pakistan) in time to be spared the wholesale
butchery in Flanders during the First World War. By 1928
Basil was second-in-command of Skinner's Horse (the
Third Horse regiment) and probably held the rank of major.
As a cavalry officer and horse-loving sportsman like his
father, he naturally took an interest in and began playing
a rough, challenging, horse-mounted native game called
polo, which the English had elsewhere converted into a
genteel sport. It was his undoing. In 1930 James and
Isabel were devastated upon receiving word that their
only son had been severely injured in a polo accident and
had died of his injuries.[45]

By this time James and Isabel's Montana adventure had
been behind them for forty years and they were settling
into old age. Their lives were secure. While at Dashwoods
cottage in 1932, a summer home in the tiny community
of Bicknoller near the Somerset coast, James Lowndes
Randall passed away. Two deaths in almost as many years

were a heavy blow. Isabel evidently remained at Dashwoods, but her widowhood was brief. Attended by her youngest sister Edith, Isabel FitzHerbert Randall passed away in mid-November 1933. She was seventy-three.[46]

In the intervening years, the quarter section of Montana property the Randalls once owned has been carved into smaller parcels, suitable for modern ranchettes. Though the original three-room cabin was gone, the log addition made to the cabin was still standing and in relatively good condition when Merrill Burlingame photographed it in 1933. This part of the house, which Isabel took such pains to decorate in 1884, stood until 1977, when, dilapidated beyond repair, it was pulled down. The stone dairy collapsed into a heap of stones in the early 1990s, and Isabel's garden is now a man-made pond.[47] As of the date of this edition, only the cottonwood tree that stood outside her parlor window—where Jem wanted to hang a beef carcass—still stands.

The pseudonymous original version of Mrs. Randall's letters disguised her identity more successfully for modern readers than it did for her contemporaries. In the past hundred years some erroneous assumptions have grown up around Isabel Randall and her book, errors that are corrected herein. Careful readers will note some changes and additions adopted to make this edition clearer for the modern reader. Names that she dropped out have been reinserted where they were positively known, and identifications are suggested where possible. Dates, which her book gives only as month and day, have had the proper year appended. Spelling, punctuation, and grammar have been left as they appeared in her book, which accounts for the odd phrasing and word constructions scattered throughout. Isabel Randall's book may have gotten her into trouble with the neighbors, but for us over a century later it is a delightful read. The text is chatty and confidential. Even the details of a log fire, which would have been unheard of outside the drawing rooms of the wealthiest country estates, were worth noticing. At a time when much writing was dense and formal, her letters glow with the excitement of a young woman overcoming challenges, learning new things, and finding pleasure in life in an unfamiliar but exciting place.

A Lady's Ranche Life

in Montana.

BY

I. R.

LONDON:

W. H. ALLEN & CO., 13, WATERLOO PLACE,
PALL MALL, S.W.

1887.

Title page from the original publication of *A Lady's Ranche Life in Montana*. Courtesy the Montana Historical Society, Helena.

Preface

This is an age of Emigration. We are sending out our sons, and brothers, our cousins, our friends, and even our daughters and sisters, to all parts of the world; or, if we are not yet sending them we are debating whether we shall send them, and so we begin to feel the want of a kind of emigration catechism; but it is easier to draw upon the questions for such a catechism than to find the proper answers; questions enough there are which we are ready to ask of those who have gone out. "What sort of country is it that you have gone to? Is it cold or hot—beautiful, or bare—healthy or unhealthy? How do you live there? What do you do? What do you get to eat? How do you spend your time? Can you get servants, or must you do all the work yourself? Can you earn a living? Must you have capital to start with, or can you work your way up to a livelihood without an allowance from home? What sort of people do you live with? are they all cowboys, or ruffians, or desperados; or are there any neighbours that you would care to have as companions, or even to welcome as friends? Is the life a very hard one? Do you really enjoy it, or do you heartily wish yourselves at home again?" There are other still more important questions to be asked: "Does the Church do her duty to her children in those far-off lands, and minister to them, and provide them with all those helps to a good and holy life, never more needed than where men are struggling for the very means of existence, and never more welcomed than by many an emigrant?" We wish we could say the Church at home has at all risen to the feeling that it is indeed one of her highest duties to provide for the spiritual needs of the thousands that leave our shores for foreign lands. Certainly no nobler work could be found for the brave young hearts and eager spirits of those who leave our English homes, than the ministering to the bands of settlers, and anyone who undertook that work would find more than enough to cheer him in brightening, strengthening, encouraging, purifying, and ennobling the hearts and characters of our emigrants. If little trace of an answer to this supreme question, "What does the Church do for you?" can be found in the pages of this little book, it is because no satisfactory answer can be given. To the other questions, and to many more besides, answers will be found in the Letters which the book contains. The Letters were written to friends at home by a young bride who went out with her husband immediately after her marriage. They are a faithful and unvarnished Record of a Settler's Life. We find in them a description of the daily record of work. There were hardships to bear, and struggles to be made. What we should chiefly gather from the Letters is that the firmness, and determination, and courage which go to form the English character will carry even those who come from the comforts of an English home well through the hardships and the struggles. The life pictured in these pages was certainly not a gloomy one. There is in it abundance of the charm of beauty of country, of genial companionship, of interesting novelty of surroundings, of the excitement of adventure, of the keen sense of enjoyment that comes from finding that you are able to do for yourself what others used to do for you. There is much to amuse, and not a little to learn from this lady's letters. Even masters of our public schools may take a warning not to discourage the study of Greek, when they see how a well-worn quotation from Homer saved one of the Settlers from being hung. The mothers of our young girls may be persuaded that there are many more useless, and even harmful, studies for their daughters to engage in than the ignoble art of cooking. Our young ladies may be persuaded that the way to secure woman's rights does not lie in making themselves in dress, manner, and conversation as much like men as possible, but much more in being as much like true women as possible, in all the quickness and readiness of a woman to fit herself to new surroundings, and in all the charm of liveliness, and cheerfulness, and usefulness that makes a man's home bright. Fathers and sons alike will see how clearly these pages show that the idle, and weak, and useless, if they do little good and much harm at home, are likely to do less good, and more harm, in other countries. Above all, those who find it hard in overcrowded England to get an opening for work, may see that it can be found in other countries. There are many who find a town life dreary, and who dread its luxury and its temptations, who shrink from the office stool, and doubt whether their honesty will stand firm in the transactions of business—many who love the open life of the country—for whom mountain and wood, field and flora, clear skies and wide plains, even storm and frost, have an attraction—many who love to have for their companions the hardy and the bold, the more unsophisticated and unconventional—who long to carve out their own fortunes, even though they have something tough to carve—these, and many others, may find that there is room for all this in a Settler's life, and better still, they will find that there is room for honest industry, and brotherly fellowship, and the softening influences of gentleness and kindness, for self-denial, for the give and take of a Settler's home, for the courtesy and hospitality that fit the new country as well as the old—in short, that there is plenty of room for true manhood, upright, bold, brave, enduring, and self-restrained, and for true womanhood, tender, true, bright, gentle, and self-sacrificing, to do its work. We venture to think that none of them will turn away disappointed from "A Lady's Ranche Life in Montana."

A Lady's Ranche Life
in Montana

What quarter of the globe have not Englishmen, and even ladies, not only visited, but lived in? So, I must confess, I was hardly prepared for the blank astonishment of all my friends, when I announced my intention of settling on the slopes of the Rocky Mountains. After the first burst of astonishment, the natural question was "Where?" But on my replying "Montana," I found, in most cases, I might just as well have said the Moon, for all the information the name conveyed.

It really was a hopeless task to explain its whereabouts, when the only places known in America seem to be New York, Chicago, and the Rocky Mountains. "But, my dear," one friend after another would say, "are you really going to a place so outlandish that we have not even heard of it? Are there any white men there (for, of course, there can't be any women), or are there nothing but Indians and grisly bears? Have the natives houses, or do they live in tents and caves, and wear skins? You can't really mean to go there, it's too dreadful. Poor dear, you will most assuredly be murdered, carried off by Indians, or devoured by wild beasts!" Very encouraging, I thought to myself, but replied cheerfully, that I knew very little about it, but would write and tell them when I got there, if I could get an Indian or grisly bear to act as postman.

I need not tell you that I did start in spite of it, for here I am, and, as it seems letters *do* leave this barbarous region, I am going to tell you all about it. Of course we crossed the Atlantic in safety, and of course the captain told someone, who told someone else, who told me, that it was the worst passage on record. I only know it *was* very rough, and I was *very* glad when, after twelve days, we reached New York.[1] Wonderful city, with its Equality and Fraternity, fearful streets, elevated railways and gigantic hotels.

Even on the wharf I found myself regarded by the Custom House officials with a kind of wondering pity. They seemed to think it their duty to find out all about me, and enlivened their disagreeable talks by brisk conversation. "Going to Montana, I see,"—looking at the labels. "Going on a trip? Going to live there, perhaps? Well, I do say." And at last, when the luggage had been turned upside down, the examining official bade me farewell and wished me good luck in my new home, as though I were going on a forlorn hope to the North Pole.

Leaving New York, we made the usual tour to the wonders of Niagara, and so on to Chicago. Of course we were assailed by the usual army of railway fiends—book, fruit, and pea-nut sellers; one of the former saying "Well, if you don't want to buy any books, just *read* this; it's awful good." Chicago I found to be, as they say in the West, "quite a place." Plenty of white men here, at any rate; and such beautiful shops with quite the latest Paris fashions. An old friend of Jem's drove us round the boulevards and parks in the neatest of stanhopes, with a pair of horses which I fell quite in love with.[2] And oh! the new racing club—an infant Sandown. Such a charming place, with its great cool verandah and *such* a lovely ball-room.[3] It made me quite loth to leave the city of cattle, cable-cars, and tinned meat manufacturer, *en route* for St. Paul.

There surely, I thought, there will be Indians and mud huts, gamblers and miners in picturesque costumes, desperadoes with silver-mounted revolvers and bowie-knives; in short, all the accessories of the frontier. Nothing of the kind; only Chicago on a smaller scale. Yet many people must recollect St. Paul as I had imagined it, and that not so very many years ago.[4] But as we took our places on the Northern Pacific Pulman car, booked for the Far West, thick and fast came visions of buffalo and grisly bear, and many a stirring encounter with that "terror of the West"; in imagination I could hear the wild yell as Crow and Piegan, Snake and Blackfoot, met in furious onslaught, and scalped one another with relentless ferocity.

"Tickets, please." Oh! What a shattering illusion! Can I really be going to the Far West? Can it really be as wild as my friends pictured it, when the journey is so easily accomplished, and travelling brought to such a pitch of perfection, as regards comfort, as it is on these Pulman cars.

At Dickenson I really did think I was getting West when the advent of our train was signalled by a salvo of revolver shots from a knot of men in broad-brimmed hats, blue shirts, and such funny leather leggings, with leather fringes down each side.[5] Jem informed me these were cowboys; and very fine, handsome men some of these "boys" were; but I should have liked them quite as well if they had left those horrid "shooting-irons," as the call them, at home. After a few hours the train reached Minquesville, where I was further surprised by a new development of cowboy. The train stopped, and in swaggered two men, dressed to the highest pitch of cowboy dandyism, accompanied by a *lady,* dressed in a dark travelling suit of the latest fashion, while her companions were adorned with the usual broad-brimmed white buckskin hat, blue shirts, embroidered brown velvet coats, a red handkerchief round their waists, with silver-mounted revolvers stuck in them, embroidered buckskin leggings with very long fringes and, to complete the equipment, a huge pair of silver Mexican spurs. Here, I thought really are a couple of true desperados of the frontier; but I was quite at a loss to account for the presence of the lady, for such she evidently was. Had she been travelling in the wild West, fallen in love with this bold frontiersman, and married him?—for I caught the glimpse of a wedding-ring, which I thought looked very bright and new. However, while I was lost in these speculations the conductor shouted "All aboard," and one of my desperados, nodding good-night to his fellow, left the train; nor did he fail to fire a parting salute as we left the station. I pondered over the lady and the cowboy, and at last concluded that they were starting on their wedding tour, and that this was the sequel to some romantic story. But I racked my brains in vain to account for it, till the black porter put up the berths for the night.

In the morning Jem told me he had most exciting intelligence, and proceeded to tell me that he had learnt, in the smoking-room, the story of the cowboy's bride; but alas! it dispelled my illusions; she had done no more than I had done myself. The two cowboys proved to be French noblemen, formerly in the French Army, who had married two English girls and were now living at their ranche in Southern Montana, enjoying the free, wild life in this glorious exhilarating air, and amassing fortunes from the increase in their flocks and herds. Jem also told me there were several French gentlemen married and settled in this part of the country.[6]

By this time the train was entering the magnificent valley of the Yellowstone, and I was well content to sit and gaze at the wonderful beauty of the scene. The clearness and brightness of the atmosphere gave a vividness to everything that I had never seen elsewhere. The golden yellow of the grass, the bright red of the brush by the riverside, the blue-black of the masses of pine against the snow, last, and perhaps most beautiful of all, the dazzling white of the snow-mountains, rising up peak above peak into the brilliant blue of this Western sky—all this formed a picture not to be excelled for brilliancy of colouring, and I began to think that this was fairyland. Perhaps it is this wonderful brightness of colour, almost as much as the geysers and other marvels of this beautiful region, that has earned for it the name of "Wonderland."[7]

And so we were carried smoothly along the blue waters of the Yellowstone, past incipient "cities" of one "store" and a "saloon," past log-cabins and "corrals," and their mean-looking headquarters of great cattle kings, counting their cattle by the thousand; past bunches of sleek, fat cattle, who lived apparently on air (so scanty did the grass appear to my uneducated eyes), past an occasional herd of startled antelope, until we took our last lingering

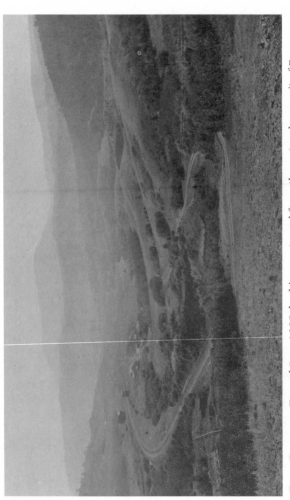

"From Boseman Tunnel," ca. 1885, looking eastward from the natural summit of Bozeman Pass, showing the railway's double track approaching the tunnel and the winding earlier wagon road. Courtesy the Montana Historical Society, Helena (940–321).

look at this lovely river and struck off across the open prairie for the Great Divide between the valleys of the Gallatin and Yellowstone. After ascending the slopes of the Divide, amidst most lovely scenery, we at last entered the Bozeman tunnel; and I must confess to an uncomfortable feeling at the thought of having the main range of the [mighty] Rockies over my head.[8] But we emerged safely at the Bozeman end, and, after admiring the pretty little town, with its odd mixture of small wooden villas and imposing brick structures, steamed slowly out into the famous Gallatin Valley—famous at least in Montana and to all who have heard of Montana, and famous to me, for this is to be my home, amongst the mountains, the cattle, the Indians, and the grisly bears.

"Moreland is the next stop," said the conductor; so as we approached our destination we stood on the platform, between the cars, to see what it looked like. A few buildings, but all very nicely built, met the eye, placed in the midst of a level valley, some eight miles long by six wide, surrounded on all sides by mountains—a veritable park. A few small white farm-houses here and there, and beautiful rivers, with their fringes of trees on both sides. "Prettiest town site in Montana, and the choicest tract of land in the best valley in the territory," says Jem enthusiastically.[9] "Jump out, here we are!"

It was Friday evening when we arrived, after two and a half days' journey from St. Paul, and we were met at the station, or "depôt," as it is called, by Jem's brother Frank, with the buggy. Mrs. Flowers, the leader of fashion in Moreland, was at the station to welcome us (so there are women here!).[10] Jem and I drove down home over ditches and badger holes, until we came to a large gate, which is

A view almost due south over downtown Manhattan, Montana—formerly Moreland—in 1892. The road crossing the track going left turned east and passed the Randall property a mile or so out of town. The better-traveled road parallel to the tracks followed them southeast to Central Park, Belgrade, and Bozeman. Courtesy the Gallatin County Historical Society & Pioneer Museum, Bozeman, Montana.

the entrance into our domain. Down a steep hill, like the side of a railroad embankment, and here we are at the door. The house is really pretty; when we have got all the things up, it will be lovely. I will give you a thorough description of it when all is done. I bought a sofa, small arm-chair, and music-stand at Chicago. Our party consists of our two selves, Jem's brother Frank, his friend B—, and our domestics; an old English couple, by name Morris, and their boy Johnny, whom Jem unearthed in the wilds of Battersea.[11] Mrs. Morris is nice and quiet, and a good cook. We are living on antelope, wild duck, fish, and prairie chicken.

I spent my first morning unpacking my big box. Nothing broken, except one small picture. I have been unpacking ever since I arrived, and have not a quarter done yet. We have breakfast at 7 A.M., luncheon at 1, and so on; Mrs. Morris cooks, and I lay the table. The boys are so pleased with knives and forks again! The weather is lovely, except in the mornings, when we have fires all over the house. On Saturday I had a tea-party; Harry, a cousin of Jem's, and Mr. H—, who rode over from his place, twelve miles off.[12]

I think I shall enjoy my life immensely, and only wish you could all be here. On Sunday we all walked to church, which was held in the parlour at the Moreland Hotel.[13] The parson gave us a long sermon, and we had the usual evening service. The hymns were rather ludicrous; one woman started them, and the rest made a noise. Our walk there was exciting, the night being pitch dark, and we had three or four streams to cross. I managed to clear them all. I have not seen any *wild beasts* yet, though I've seen plenty of cowboys. We are only a mile from the *town* (eight houses and an hôtel); but only think, in this barbarous region, being only a mile from railway station, telegraph, and post-office! It almost reads like the advertisement of an English country home.[14]

October 27th. [1884]

I have been busy all this week cleaning and dusting the house. I find there are a good many household things to be got, so we are going to Bozeman (eighteen miles by road, or three-quarters of an hour by train) to get them. The drawing-room and bed-room will be as nice and pretty as can be wished, with curtains, carpets, &c., but the dining-room will have to wait. Jem and I made a towel-horse; it looks grand, but he hasn't time for much of that sort of thing.

One afternoon we drove up to the horse-ranche, and saw a band of fifty or sixty horses corralled. We were just in time to see them all come galloping down from the hills; the men got them in very cleverly. I have ridden three times on a very quiet mare, Truemaid; she is the last Jem broke, just four years old. The saddle I got from Griffiths and MacDougall fits her very well. My *race-horse,* Daisy, came back from her trainer's yesterday. She is a real beauty, fit to ride in the Park, and very showy. I hope I shall be able to use her. Another day we rode up to the horse-ranche and saw Jem and Frank branding colts. It was most exciting. They are driven into the corral, a sort of yard, generally round, with a fence seven feet high made of strong poles laid one on top of the other between very strong posts. Then the colts are lassoed by the front feet and thrown. One man jumps on their heads, to keep them down, while the other holds their fore-feet off the ground with a lasso, and a third brands them. It seems such a shame, branding the poor little things, and is a great disfigurement afterwards; but, of course, it is quite unavoidable, as the horses out here all run together in the hills, like New Forest or Exmoor ponies.[15]

All the Englishmen out here have been to call.[16] I have had a visitor every day, and sometimes two. Mrs. Morris is very willing to work and we get on very well. I work in the house all the morning, and am out with Jem or the boys all the afternoon; we play whist every evening. The two boys have started on a week's hunt, and hope to bring back no end of game. We breakfast on trout and whitefish, which we catch every morning, and dine off wild duck, teal, and prairie chicken, the latter as good as grouse, only bigger.[17] I am writing by a log fire, which is too warm, as the sun has come out. The weather is perfect, bright sunny days and cold nights. I think that the air here is quite as good as in Derbyshire, only drier. My piano hasn't come yet, so the drawing-room is left undone; but the photographs and pictures are gradually going up, and look well on the red paper. There was a ball ten or twelve miles from here the other evening; and I heard that the dancing was really not bad. You will hear of me going to one soon.

November 2nd. [1884]

We went to Bozeman on Tuesday, started at 10 A.M. and got back at 8:30, the train being four hours late owing to a mass of rock having fallen on the line. Bozeman is a nice little town of about 3,000 inhabitants; there are some rather pretty Swiss-looking villas, which are the residences of the principal business men. The main street, which is generally six inches deep in either dust, mud, or snow,

A VIEW FROM SAFE QUARTERS.

An illustration from Brisbin's *The Beef Bonanza* (1881), "A View from Safe Quarters," implicitly demonstrating to readers like James and Isabel Randall how safe it was for women to participate along the edges of the western livestock industry's wealth-building.

had some good brick and stone buildings, and boasts of two villainous hotels, but in the stores (*Anglice,* shops) you can get any conceivable thing you want, except, perhaps, a Paris bonnet or the last number of the *Queen.* We did our shopping satisfactorily. Could anything be nicer than to start after breakfast, get through all our shopping and be back again by 5 o'clock? I felt exactly as if we had been up to London and back for the day.

We are having a very pleasant week all to ourselves, as the boys are away. One day Jem and I started at 10 A.M., after

An overview of Bozeman, Montana, in 1894, from the northeast. Photograph by F. Jay Haynes. Courtesy the Haynes Foundation Collection, Montana Historical Society, Helena (H 3179).

my work was done, to hunt for cattle. I rode Daisy; she is perfect. Jem has given her to me as a wedding present; and no one else is ever to ride her. She is very showy, and "high lifed," nearly thoroughbred, or "gently raised," as they call it. Some day I may get to riding "bronchos," *i.e.* native horses, which run wild in the hills till they are old enough to break. We did not find the cattle, but had a lovely ride of twenty miles. We had coffee, bread and butter, and buffalo-berry jelly (which is as good as red currant), at a small ranche, and all sat down together with the men. The women waited on us; they were very polite to me, but seemed to look on me as a kind of wild animal.[18] We got back in time for 5 o'clock tea. Mrs. Morris is not strong, but gets on very well. I do all the housemaiding and parlourmaiding.

November 10th. [1884]

I really must tell you about our lady callers, for you will have found out by this time that the grisly bears and the Indians are all a myth, that we are living quite a hum- drum existence in the midst of the highest civilization, and that life in the Far West at the present day is by no means a succession of stirring adventures by flood and field.[19] My first caller was the lady (they are all *ladies* out here) who supplies us with butter.[20] She came down about 11 o'clock one morning with some butter, and I received her in the kitchen, where we conversed amicably until she took her departure. This, as we afterwards learnt, gave dire offence. It was a *bonâ fide* morning call, and I ought to have received her ladyship in the "parlour" with my best company manners.

Our next callers arrived one afternoon in a buggy; I basely fled, and left Jem to do the honours. As he had not much cultivated the acquaintance of the softer sex out here, he hadn't the least idea who they were. However, he asked them to come in and sit down, which they did side by side on two chairs, with their backs against the wall; they were got up, as he said, "quite regardless" in feathers and warpaint—literally the latter. Imagine a countenance, to which the sun of Montana had already been kind, plentifully smeared with rouge and pearl-powder. I find this is a common practice out here, learned, I suppose, from the Indians. On leaving they left *cards* for me in the most orthodox style, as we discovered that they represented the *crême de la crême* of the society of the neighbourhood.

Jem says he is afraid that I shall not find any more of my own sex very congenial companions—in fact, very much the reverse—but in time, perhaps, the country may get more thickly settled with English people, or a better class of Americans from the older States.[21] We have made some feeble attempts to get up lawn tennis and cricket among the English, but so far without much success. As they say, "A man doesn't want to hunt for exercise in this country, where he is hard at work from morning til dewy eve." It seems ludicrous to look back on English life, and the oft-recurring question "What shall we do to-day?" when here it is not a question of "*What* shall we do?" but "How in the world will we find time to do it all?"

Two afternoons we spent in buffalo-berrying and shooting combined. The novel way of picking this fruit is to cut down huge branches from the bushes, and then beat them with a stick; the berries shower down into a sheet, spread out on the ground.[22] In this way we soon gather all we want. Every now and then prairie chicken or grouse make their appearance upon the scene, or a duck goes down upon the pool close by, and rush is made for the gun; so that the entertainment is of a varied nature.

My drawing-room is lovely. I have put up the four red curtains on each side of the two side windows, and the looking-glass between, photograph frames and writing-table underneath. The other outside wall has one window with red curtains. I will finish the description when my piano comes, as the room is not a quarter done yet. Now for the wild beasts! just in from a walk I saw a white weasel, a chip monk, a pretty little beast with black and white stripes down its back (something between a squirrel and a rat), and a white-tailed deer.[23]

November 23rd. [1884]

Last week Jem and I started at 8 o'clock to ride to Three Forks (a ranche belonging to some English friends), to buy horses for the Eastern market.[24] It was a ride of about 12 miles. When we were half way there, we met one of the owners of the ranche coming to see us; he stopped and made us promise to stay the night, while he went on to our place to fetch our things. Three Forks is a nice place, and the house very comfortably furnished. As it was being cleaned, we were quartered at the hotel close by. After supper we came into the "parlour" and found half the population, working men and all, assembled to inspect the "stranger." The only female in the room immediately undertook to introduce me all round, which appears to be the custom out here; the ceremony being effected by a general hand-shaking with the accompanying expression, "Glad to make your acquaintance, Ma'am."

We rode home the next morning through the foothills. The ground was, of course, frozen as hard as a brick, so it was not very good "going." It never is out here, for that matter, as the ground is either as hard as a rock from frost or drought, or else covered with snow, or sticky as glue from wet. The hills were all covered with dry tufts of yellow-looking grass; most unappetizing fodder, I should think; but stock live and thrive on it all the winter, pawing and rooting through the light snow. Jem says it is cured by the sun as it stands, in July, and is really like the very best hay, preserved with all the juices in it.

When we got back, we found the boys had come home from their hunt, with a waggon-load of sage hens and small game, but alas! no elk or deer to show for their pains.[25]

We are beginning the real cold weather now. Everything freezes in the house at night. The bread is like a cannon ball, meat and everything else in the same condition, and the milk a block of ice. In our bed-room, though we had a fire in the room over night, we found the water in the bath frozen solid to the bottom. I rode in the middle of the day and did not feel the cold in the least; though Jem's beard and moustache were a mass of ice, and icicles hung from the horses' noses, while their bodies were covered with frost. I suppose one does not feel the cold because the air is so dry at this altitude, 3,000 feet above the level of the sea; also because there is no wind, and the sun is always bright. Yesterday the thermometer was 12 deg. below zero at noon, and yet I didn't think it was nearly so cold as it is when we have 10 degs. of frost at home. This "storm," as they call the spell of cold weather, lasted about 10 days; the thermometer at night is going down to 30 below zero.

To-day the "Chinook" wind is blowing, the roofs are dripping, the birds twittering and splashing in the puddles, horses galloping about, squealing and kicking up their heels; we have got all the windows open, and it is like spring. This Chinook wind is the warm current of air, which comes roaring, salt laden from the Pacific, melting the snow and changing the depth of winter into spring in a few hours. It is the stockman's best friend, and enables his stock to withstand the rigours of winter without shelter and with no food, except what nature provides in the shape of the dried grasses in the hills.

The thaw brought us three visitors, Englishmen, who rode over to lunch. Of course we were very glad to see them, and it felt very homelike. However, we were suddenly reminded of where we were, by hearing the harsh notes of wild geese flying over the house, and made a rush for the rifles; a volley resulting in the death of one goose, which came down with a tremendous thud. A great big Canada goose, weighing nearly 20 lbs.[26]

December 2nd. [1884]

Since the thaw, I have been almost living in the saddle, riding about with Jem, hunting for two very valuable well-bred mares, which have disappeared. I have been over and through the most awful places; quaking bogs, wide rivers, very rapid and almost deep enough to swim a horse, and through brush which nearly drags one off one's horse. The marvel is that I'm alive to tell the tale. The worst of it is, we have not found the mares; and on arriving home, there was a report that two noted horse-thieves had been found, camping in the brush, about a mile from here, and that the man, who saw them, had pulled his six-shooter on them, but that they had disappeared in the brush. If they have taken our mares and any others have gone from near here, I suppose a posse of men will pursue them and there will be a fight, and the attendance of "Judge Lynch" will be requested.

They are very much "down" on horse-thieves. Of course I am very sorry for the poor men, but horse-stealing seems to be on the increase and must be put down. It is so easy for the thieves to get away with their plunder in this country. Jem says, last year a posse of men, well armed, pursued one gang of horse-thieves, and, after a pitched battle, were beaten off, and the thieves remained masters of the field. Perhaps it is not so civilized here after all.

To return to peaceful subjects. You will wonder, perhaps, what we burn out here. There are any amount of cotton-wood trees on our ranche, and the other day we had the steam saw down here, and sawed up enough to last the whole winter.[27] We have such glorious fires, with great logs three and a half feet long, and as big around as a man's body, piled half-way up the chimneys. There are only two rooms with big fire-places, the drawing-room and Jem's den. All the other rooms are heated with stoves, and it almost keeps one man busy, sawing and splitting billets of wood for them.

While they were all busy with the steam saw, I got on Daisy and rode round to see that all the young stock and "bonny brood-mares" were safe. We keep all our best horses close to the ranche for fear of horse-thieves, and I must confess I was in terror, all the time I was out, of meeting some of these gentry, after the report we had heard.

Instead of gates out here, they generally have bars, which you have to let down; and as I could not get off, I amused myself with letting down the top bar and jumping the balance, like the "heave gates" in Sussex. Daisy jumped very well indeed. I should like to ride her out hunting at home. All the horses were safe; my ride was most enjoyable, and I hope, after a time, to become an accomplished stock-woman.

In the evening as we sat round the fire—the boys smoking their pipes—Frank alluded to the loss of the two mares, which have never yet been found. I fear they never will be. He said he thought it was a mistake to keep good stock under fence, as these horse-thieves know exactly where to find them. He told a story of an expert horse-thief who came to a man who had an extra good lot of horses out in the hills, and warned him, in a confidential way, that there were horse-thieves about, adding, "If I were you, I should bring all my horses in and keep them in a corral at night." The unsuspecting owner acted on this advice. The next night the horse-thieves came, let down the bars, and drove off the whole lot, no doubt feeling much obliged to the owner for gathering the band for them.

December 5th. [1884]

I have been experimenting in cooking lately, as there is no knowing what may happen in a country where servants are so few and far between, and so very independent. I made a lot of those Rock Cakes which I learnt to make at South Kensington. The boys gobbled them up in no time. My next venture was pancakes; and the crowning success, ox-foot jelly. We got the feet from a "beef" which we killed the other day. This is our winter supply of beef.

Just fancy, in England getting a whole bullock at a time! Jem wanted to hang it up on a tree just in front of the drawing-room window, saying, "it would be handy when we wanted a steak"; but on this I had to put my veto. Really one could not have that object always in front of one's eyes, and watch it disappearing during the winter. You see it will freeze now and keep till spring, and be cut up as we want it. Beef brings me to potatoes. Montana produces the best in the world; so floury, and the size astounding; some of them weigh four pounds apiece, and one is enough for four people.

December 9th. [1884]

Another cold spell set in yesterday and the cold is intense. I like it, and find I can stand it much better than the men; while they are frozen, I am comparatively warm.

We have been living, until the last few days, on baking-powder bread, but everyone told us it was unwholesome; so the other day Mrs. Morris went to a neighbour's house to learn how to make yeast.[28] Her first batch of yeast bread was a lump of lead, and nearly *black*; so I tried *my* hand. My bread *was* white, and comparatively light. Last night I made a lemon pudding for dinner. It came out a most beautiful mould; not a bit heavy. We get plenty of milk and cream from our one cow, but now go without butter as it is expensive to buy.[29] Game and meat we bake in our American cooking-stove, which does them very well. I always make the puddings in the morning, so as to have them ready by dinner-time.

You ask about our domestics. Mrs. Morris is tolerably cheerful and hard-working. [Mr.] Morris is slow, but always seems to be pottering about doing something; and Johnnie is useful in odd jobs, cleaning knives, boots, &c. On the whole, considering they come from the slums of London, and how little we knew about them, they have turned out better than could have been expected.

Frank and I always wash up after luncheon and dinner, as Mrs. Morris never gets the things as clean as she might do. They always put soap in the water to wash dishes, &c., out here, which was a novelty to me; however, Frank had learned that in his bachelor days, and put me up to it.

December 23rd. [1884]

Since I last wrote we have had our first heavy snowfall to a depth of from eighteen to twenty inches; it is hard on the stock out of doors, and a great plague to me indoors, as the house gets so dirty; and, to make matters worse, Mrs. Morris has got a bad foot, and is *hors de combat,* so I have to do everything. Luckily, as it is snowing so hard, the men can't go out much, so they all help me. Frank is a capital cook, and helps me a great deal.

Our Christmas party has had to be put off—a great disappointment, as it is an engagement of a year's standing. Some of the Englishmen from Three Forks were coming, but the storm is so bad that they could not easily get here. The Christmas pudding is achieved—a great triumph, as we all had a hand in it. Frank and I cut up the suet, and we all amused ourselves one evening stoning the raisins; I stirred all the ingredients up in a large tin basin, and it smells quite the proper thing. Frank has just come running in, and flourishing a huge piece of beef in my face with great glee. It is the Christmas sirloin which he and Jem have just sawn out of the frozen carcass, which I mentioned to you before.

December 30th. [1884]

Before I can begin to write this letter the ink must be put down by the fire to thaw out, as it is frozen solid. I'm getting quite used to the water freezing in my basin while I'm washing my hands, and the towels freezing stiff before I can dry them! Christmas-day was lovely. I tried walking in snow up to my knees, but stuck at last in a drift, and had to be ignominiously pulled out by main force. In the evening, if our party was not large, it was very merry. The sirloin was pronounced first-rate, and equal to the very best English beef; the pudding was a great success, light, but no crumbling, and we lit it up in due form. We toasted our absent friends in lager beer, and enjoyed ourselves generally.[30] We had all donned our best bibs and tuckers in honour of the occasion, and at last retired to the drawing-room, where I played the accompaniments to hunting songs, till everyone was hoarse. Then we fell upon Frank to tell his famous hanging story, which he did, after much pressing, to this effect:—

A few years ago, he went in the autumn to Oregon, to buy a large drove of horses to drive to Montana for sale; but on arriving there, he found the prices too high to justify the investment, so the enterprise was abandoned. He knocked about there for some months, and made the acquaintance of certain famous frontier characters, more adventurous than respectable. Amongst others the famous Hank Vaughan, who fought a desperate duel, in which the combatants clasped their left hands, and emptied their six shooters. Both men fell, but, marvelous to relate both recovered.

However to return to Frank's adventures. He was away from stores and civilization a good deal: at one time with

the Umatilla Indians, and at another in the mining camps in
the mountains, and so gradually his appearance resem-
bled that of a Western desperado, or "bad man," much
more than an Oxford graduate.[31] In the spring, he started
on horseback for Montana. Unfortunately for him, as it
eventually turned out, on the same day, from the same
place, and on a horse of the same colour, started a well-
known desperado, who had robbed and murdered a man
somewhere close by. The murderer travelled fast—naturally; so did Frank, for some reason or another, and both
being well mounted, they made about the same distances
each day.

Meanwhile a description of the murderer had been
sent forward, and the Sheriff started, from some point
down the trail, to intercept him. Early one morning
Sheriff and murderer met.

"Throw up your hands," shouted the Sheriff.

"Read your warrant," was the murderer's cool reply.

As the unfortunate Sheriff lowered his pistol to draw
the warrant from his pocket, quick as a flash the murderer shot him dead, and galloped off.

For some days Frank, quite unconscious of the double
tragedy that had been enacted, pursued the same route
as the murderer. At one place they both exchanged their
tired horses for fresh ones. Soon after this they must have
taken different routes, and Frank arrived at a noted mining
city. Strolling through town, he was pointed out to the
Sheriff as the Oregon murderer. He had sold or lost his
revolver, and the empty scabbard hung at his belt. The
Sheriff observing this, and knowing the desperate character
of the man for whom Frank was mistaken, supposed he
had his pistol concealed, and ready for immediate use.

Consequently he deemed, I suppose, discretion the better part of valour, and went off in search of the Deputy-Sheriff to make the arrest.

Meanwhile the pseudo murderer mounted his horse, and cantered gaily along his journey. After riding some miles, he was suddenly aware of a horse galloping rapidly up behind him, and heard a shout:

"Throw up your hands!"

Not being of a nervous disposition, he treated the summons as a joke, and commenced some jocular reply, which was rudely cut short by the ugly sight of a pistol pointed at his head; whereupon he hastily did as he was bid, and threw up his hands. The next second he dropped his right hand, intending to produce his empty scabbard as a proof of being unarmed, which ill-advised movement nearly cost him his life. In fact, after his arrest the Deputy-Sheriff told him that it was little short of a miracle that he did not instantly shoot him, when he dropped his hand, believing him, of course, to be a desperate character, and that he had dropped his hand to seize the pistol, which is usually carried in the scabbard on the belt round the man's waist.

Frank's next move was to ask the Sheriff to read his warrant; which he did, with his eye and a pistol on Frank; giving the warrant extempore without running his eye over the document. He had already heard of the fate of the former Sheriff, and did not intend to be caught by the same manoeuvre. Frank then quietly gave himself up, at the same time asserting his innocence. The Sheriff then proceeded to handcuff him and turned the horses' heads towards the town.

On the way they stopped at a "cow" camp, where there were several of the boys. These learnt the supposed crime of the prisoner. Without more ado, they decided to constitute themselves judge, jury, and executioner; the insecurity of Western prisons having been so often demonstrated, it is not surprising that men often want to take the law into their own hands in the case of a desperate character. In vain Frank chaffed, stormed, and expostulated in turn; at last he said, if they would question him, they would find he was not, and could not possibly be the man they took him for. They seemed to be struck with the idea that it would be rather good fun to cross-examine the prisoner, and a well-educated man promptly accepted the *role* of counsel for the prosecution.

"Where were you in '81?"

"I was in Canada."

"Where were you in '80?"

"I was in Montana."

Our real murderer, an uneducated ruffian, had come from Texas, and had honoured Oregon ever since. Something of his history was probably known to the jury.

"Where were you in '79?"

"I was at the University at Oxford."

A derisive cheer followed this announcement.

"You at a University, a hard-looking citizen like you! Anything else? Tell that to the marines" (or whatever represents that useful body in the West).

"Hard-looking citizen or not," said Frank, boldly, "I tell you I was there."

A bright idea seemed to strike the counsel for the prosecution.

"Well," he said; "if you were at any university you must have learnt something. What books did you read?"

"Oh," said Frank, feeling a love for the names of those authors which had never before inspired him, "Livy, Virgil, Homer, Aeschylus, Euripides, and, and—"

Looks were exchanged, and our cowboy friends began to think that there might be some mistake.

"Quote some Latin," said the counsel for the prosecution, "and you are a free man."

"Propria quae maribus, Πολυφλοισβοιο θαλασσης."[32]

Never did the words sound so sweet to human ear. Out of the recesses of his memory this was all he could drag to light at the moment. But that was enough. Handcuffs off, apology from the Sheriff, drinks all round; and once, at any rate, in the annals of history, an Oxford education had proved of value in the Rocky Mountains. This roughly, as far as I can remember, was Frank's story, and I think you will acknowledge that it was a strange experience enough. By this time the huge Yule log was nearly reduced to ashes, the clock had chimed the small hours more than once, so we reluctantly brought our first Christmas in the Rockies to a close. I went to bed to dream that a hoarse voice was ordering me to throw up my hands, but they remained glued to my side. Next that the rope was already around my neck, and I was ordered, on pain of instant death, to quote a page of Racine, which, needless to say, memory refused to recall.

Next morning the cold was simply fearful. Morris informed Jem "that it was pretty sharp this morning." Pretty sharp! I should think it was. The thermometer registered 59° below zero, or 91° of frost, and your phlegmatic Englishman opines that "it is pretty sharp." As for me, I tried to do some house-cleaning, and got hotache in my hands whenever I moved away from the fire. Mrs. Morris wisely stayed in bed and left me to manage as best I could. The clock was frozen on Christmas night, and stopped. Now, as I write this, the Chinook wind is blowing and it is as mild as spring.

January 4th. [1885]

You say my letters don't come very regularly. I write every week; but we often don't send to the post-office for days at a time during a cold spell. Mrs. Morris has recovered, and she and I between us have got the house thoroughly cleaned; it smells so fresh and nice. I have been staining the floor of our little dressing-room, and putting up red curtains; it looks very cosy. The Chinook is still roaring away, and the snow going rapidly, the air is so soft and delicious. When I was out the other day I observed millions of little black insects on the snow; so when I got home I suggested that the Chinook brought these insects, and that they devoured the snow, which accounted for its disappearance.[33] This observation on natural history was not received with the respect which its originality deserved.

Mrs. Flowers lent me a whole heap of books the other day, but I've not much time for reading.[34] Frank and I have gone in for a course of Shakespeare this winter, whom we cannot make Jem appreciate; he still sticks to his Tennyson, and such lighter stuff.

The other day a beautiful gilt-edged card came by post, which proved to be an invitation to a bachelor's ball in Bozeman; the committee of management consisting of all our tradespeople; I don't think we shall go, but it is kind of them to ask us. Jem says that the usual practice with regard to balls is, for every bachelor for miles round to engage "his girl" for the evening. He has to drive her to the ball, dance with her all evening, provide her with supper, and drive her home afterwards.

January 20th. [1885]

We are rejoicing in another cold spell and a very heavy snowfall; as the old snow had not half melted when the fresh fall came, the snow is about two feet deep. To add to our misery, everyone in the house, except me, is suffering from what they call mountain fever. I have doctored them all out of my medicine chest, and hope they will soon recover.

Last time I went out, Jem took his gun and we went scrambling about in the deep snow, hunting for game; but only got a pheasant (something resembling a grouse more than a pheasant, only its meat is white when cooked) and a couple of rabbits.[35] Suddenly Jem stopped and told me to come up quickly; when I saw a large grey wolf close to us, slinking away as fast as he could. He looked an awful coward, and much afraid of us. These large grey wolves are luckily rare, as they do a great deal of damage amongst young colts and calves. Government pays a bounty of, I think, ten shillings a head for their destruction. This is the first wild animal I've seen, except antelope and white-tailed deer. I'm afraid there are no bears about here.

January 26th. [1885]

This week we made a huge snowball to represent wickets, and made snow cricket-balls, as hard as a brick, and used my tennis racquets as a bat. Of course, we could not move about much, as the snow was so deep;

still it was pretty good fun. Amusement is rather scarce just now, as the snow is so deep, and the cold is too great to allow of driving or riding.

I've been trying to instil tidiness and cleanliness into Mrs. Morris. She is very willing, but *very* dirty and untidy. One advantage of this couple is that they have been used to such poverty that they don't expect much, which is just as well out here. Still, I hope some day to be able to have rather a better class of people. We had pancakes made with snow the other day, instead of eggs; Jem pronounced them "ripping." I had heard of people making them in Russia with snow, and wanted to try them.

It's a great shame the way some people neglect their cattle out here. Those which are right back in the hills where the grass is good do well enough; but those which are down among the settlements, where feed is so scarce, ought to be fed. A small bunch of all ages, from a six month' calf to very old cows, comes past here every day. They make furious attacks on our hay corral; even barbed wire hardly stops them, and they get terribly cut trying to get through. I feel very sorry for them, but of course we can't feed them, as all the hay is wanted for our horses. What these cattle live on is a mystery. Certainly they pick over the litter which is thrown out of our stable; that and the dry twigs is all they can possibly get. It will be interesting to watch if they get through the winter. If they *do,* I'm sure no one need ever be afraid of cattle not making their own living out here all the year round.

I saw in the *Field* the other day, that an English farmer had got three weeks' imprisonment for starving a cow. I shrewdly suspect that a good many Montana cattle-men would spend their whole lives in prison at that rate.

January 31st. [1885]

The Morrises are getting very independent and trouble-some; I can hardly get any work out of Mrs. Morris, and I expect we shall have to part with them. They are talking of going, and I for one shan't miss them; I've had to show Mrs. Morris how to do everything, and generally done the cooking myself. Only fancy, Mrs. Flowers asked them to tea with her. How can anyone keep servants in their place, when the people, whom we associate with, invite them to their houses as equals?

We had a delicious ride the other day. The weather has changed since I last wrote, and the snow has all gone. Jem went to buy hay, and we rode all along by the river, jumping several fences. It was really good going, and reminded one of riding over the old English pastures. I listened to Jem's bargaining, and felt glad I don't have anything of that kind to do. The people are so independent, and seem as if they would sooner keep what they have to sell, for ever, than take a penny less than they ask.

They generally put the price up the moment anyone comes to buy; then when the intending purchaser goes away disgusted, they complain that they can't sell anything, and that there is no money in the country. And yet they would act in exactly the same way if another purchaser came the next day.

Some Englishmen, who are feeding about 300 pigs on their ranche near here, are coming down with a pig for us to-day, so we shall be well off for meat.[36] The bullock we killed in November isn't nearly finished yet, so it has held out well. I think it is a great advantage living in a country where you can freeze your meat, and let it hang until you want it. With regard to the beef, Jem affords us a good deal of amusement. If a cold spell comes, he's miserable because it is so hard on the horses; if a chinook comes, he's in a state of mind about the beef for fear it should go bad. So far, there seems to be no fear of that, it takes a long time to thaw out.

To-day is the first day I've seen real mud since I've been here, it seems quite home-like; which reminds one of the British tar, who, on returning to London from the Mediterranean, exclaimed, "No more of your confounded blue skies, here's a jolly old English fog."

All our young colts have been weaned, and have been kept up in the yard for the last few weeks; they are going well, and it is a great amusement to me to pet and gentle them. The mischievous little wretches are always slipping out, and getting back to their mothers; so we have to be very careful to keep the yard gate shut.

February 8th. [1885]

As we were riding up to town the other day, we saw a waggon and horses running away; so off we went as hard as we could, plunging through snowdrifts, and stumbling into badgerholes covered by the snow, to head them. After circling them round a little while, we managed to stop them. Daisy nearly ran away with me, under the impression that she was running a race. After waiting some time, a very fat old man came waddling and puffing through the snow to claim his conveyance, and was profuse in his thanks.

I wonder there are not more runaways; they are always leaving their horses standing while they go into the saloon—or bar, as we should call it—and as they have no regular cart-horses, but all rather light, well bred, high-lifed horses, it is surprising that they stand as well as they do.

I've been occupying myself with dressmaking this week, turning and altering some old things, to wear when I'm working in the mornings.

February 22nd. [1885]

All this week the weather has been delicious; we've had no fires in the house until the evening, and *now* there are seven inches of snow. It is snowing hard, and there is no sign of its stopping.

The other day I went with Jem and Frank in the hay-rack to get a load of hay, from a stack about two miles from here. Going there I was nearly shaken to death. I do think a hay-rack is the roughest conveyance ever invented. While they were loading up, I lay on the haystack; it smelt delicious, like new-mown hay, and the sun was so warm, that I only had to close my eyes to imagine I was lying on a haycock in the middle of summer. On the way back we got a good many prairie-chicken. They are not the least suspicious of a waggon, though quite unapproachable on foot now. Frank missed one sitting on the top of a very high tree, and it actually sat there waiting to be shot at again, apparently quite innocent of where the shot came from.

A very valuable colt was running in the yard the other day, when the stupid little thing jumped a high half door into the stables and fell, dislocating its knee. None of the men could pull it in again, so they telegraphed for the doctor to come from Three Forks; he came driving at full speed and got here at six o'clock, and quickly put the poor little fellow right again, bandaging the knee with plaster-of-paris. We made the doctor stop for dinner, but he would not stay the night; he seems a very clever man to talk to, a Canadian, but likes to be thought an American. He is very well off, and has made every penny himself. I don't think I should mind being doctored by him, he is so pleasant.[37]

On Friday, Jem and I rode nearly all day, looking for two mares, which had strayed. We went up into the hills, it is the first time I have been there. No one can imagine how lovely it is until they have been there; so free and such lovely air; any number of horses, some gentle, some wild. We saw any amount of the Company's horses, and Jem was delighted to see them looking so fat and well, though how they live is a marvel to me.[38] The snow is still deep, but in places there are little bare patches with short brown grass on them (buffalo-grass Jem calls it), which is supposed to be such wonderful stuff, and it must be, or they could not do so well on it.[39]

The range is made up of beautiful deep valleys with streams of clear water always running; then flat plains, then more hills and high mountains beyond. When we were up there, we saw a jack rabbit (just like a Scotch hare, all white), and some antelope, we saw no traces of our two mares, but the boys found them yesterday.[40]

March 1st. [1885]

I have been out very little lately, except to go for hay in the waggon, as the ground is frightful with mud and water. One day this week I went out to see what Jem calls Sunday-school, which consists in putting a saddle on all the yearlings, and making Johnny ride them. One little wretch began to buck, sent Johnny off, and kicked him as she ran away. I think the boy will ride well some day, as he stuck on for two or three jumps. Then Jem got on, and there was no end of a scene; the colt bucking and bawling all round the yard, and doing her best to get him off; but, of course, he was too heavy for her to buck very hard. Then Frank came and rode one; and so they went on for about an hour. The way these horses bawl out here is most extraordinary; just like a cow or calf,—it does sound so wicked.

Our hens are beginning to lay well; we have just built a capital hen-house of logs, laid one on top of the other, with the chinks filled up with mortar; so I hope we shall get some chickens soon, when the warm weather comes. Our stock of poultry consists of about thirty or forty common barn-door fowls. The skunks and coyotes rather interfere with the increase of the fowl population; still I hope we may do pretty well with the chickens—which is my department—as Jem says this is a very good chicken ranche. The birds get their own living all the summer in the brush, and moreover the brush protects them from the large hawks, which are very destructive to chickens on the open prairie.

I think I told you that our ranche was down on the river bottom, all amongst the trees and brush.[41] This country is quite destitute of such ornaments, except on the river bottoms, though the high mountains are covered with a dense growth of pines.

The worst of chicken-farming here is, that in the summer there is a glut of eggs, when they only fetch sixpence a dozen, and are hard to sell even at that price, and the winters are, of course, too cold to allow hens to lay at all. However, eggs will be very useful in summer, when it is

most difficult to have any fresh meat, as it will not keep
more than a day or two, and out here you have to get
such a quantity at a time. It will be nice here in summer
when all the trees are out, and if we can make a lawn
round the house it will be very pretty. At present I'm
afraid English people would be much astonished at the
mess round the house. In winter, of course, nothing can
be done on account of the snow.

March 15th. [1885]

The weather is perfect now. We have tea out of doors,
on the garden seat, in front of the house. I've been riding
every day, and everything seems to be enjoying the warm
weather; all the horses are getting sleek and fat, you
never saw such a difference.

We have begun breakfast at 7:30, which Mrs. Morris
seems to think a great grievance, and has been in a very
bad temper in consequence; so I told her if we had any
more of her temper she would have to go; this threat
seems to have had good effect.

The hens are beginning to lay well, any amount of
eggs; I find them in all sorts of queer places. My worst
enemies are the magpies, who steal such numbers.[42]
They seem to know what the cackling of a hen means, as
well as I do.

Jem and Frank are busy in the evenings making a
fence all round the house, enclosing about two acres.
This is to be the fruit and flower garden, at present we
have nothing in it but rhubarb. Nearly all the old rubbish
has been cleared away, and they are planning out paths
and a drive, which is to be laid down in gravel. We can
get plenty of that from the river. We expect to make our

Home Farm of 160 acres pay for our living and domestics; but, of course, our mainstay is the horse business.

All the spring birds are arriving, so spring will soon be here, I hope. I saw some robins to day, which are like the English birds, only much larger, as big as blackbirds; and I also saw some beautiful blue birds—these only come here in the spring and summer.[43]

March 23rd. [1885]

There was an eclipse of the sun to-day; the result of which was, that it got pitch dark about 10 A.M., remained so for three-quarters of an hour and blew a hurricane all the time.[44]

I'm going into the stock business on my own account and mean to invest in a cow, as Polly has gone dry. I find it almost impossible to make puddings without milk and butter, even though we do have plenty of eggs. The South Kensington book is very useful, as there are so many simple recipes in it.[45]

We are getting lots of little pigs now, and hope they will prove profitable. Pork has been worth 5d. [five pence] a pound till this year, but, I suppose, like everything else, it will go down in price soon. Mrs. Morris is getting so fine, that she grumbles at having to eat pork, and thinks beef is to be got as easily as it is in England. Jem says Mrs. Morris won't eat pork because the pigs had been fed on horse-flesh. She got this idea into her head because the Englishmen, who are feeding 300 pigs, gave some of theirs a lot of dead horses which were smothered in a closed railway truck.

The man who shipped them put twenty in a closed truck, and eighteen of them were smothered before they had gone fifteen miles. They were thrown out close to the pig ranch, and were a great find for the pig-feeders.[46] You know I told you we got a pig from there, and so Mrs. Morris got the idea into her head that this pig had been fed of horse-flesh. If pigs never ate anything worse than good fresh horse-flesh, I, for one, should not mind. The other morning Mrs. Morris brought a piece of pork with a piece of string stuck in it, and assured me, with a long face, that this pig must have been "fed upon string."

Now that the ice is out of the river, we catch plenty of fish. The bait is generally a bit of raw meat; they won't take a fly yet. There are three kinds of fish in our river and "creek"—trout, grayling, and white fish.[47] The latter are very unsuspicious and easily caught, but not half as good eating as either of the former, and don't give half as good sport (when you are fishing for sport), as they give in directly [when] they are hooked, and you pull them out as if they were dead. When we are not fishing for sport, but only for the pot, we use a long stick and a piece of strong line, with a bit of raw meat on the hook, and jerk the fish right over our heads as soon as they bite. It is not very sportsmanlike, but very effective and expeditious.

I've been helping Jem to "fix up" fences. They use what are called "snake" fences a good deal out here, which are made without any posts, by simply laying of poles one over the other. They are called "snake" fences because they don't go straight, but form an angle where the poles overlap each other, but I thought that they had that name because they were built so that snakes could not get through.

March 29th. [1885]

We tried a new "buggy" mare the other day, and she behaved very well; trotted ten miles in an hour, and only astonished us once by kicking, and that was only in play, as she was fresh and evidently enjoyed being out. Jem thinks she's going to make a trotter.

They think more of a trotter out here than anything else, and often astonish me by saying Daisy is too good for a "saddle horse," and would make such a good "buggy" animal. Too good for a saddle horse! That seems to be rather upsetting the order of things, according to the English notion at least. But here they seem to think anything is good enough to ride, and that the pick of the flock ought to be kept for harness. It seems to me that one might define the Americans as a "driving" race.

A revolution has taken place in our establishment. The Morrises leave on Tuesday, if they can find a place to go to. I could not stand her any longer. Latterly, if I have dared to say a word as to what work she ought to do, or ventured to say the potatoes were not boiled, or anything of that sort, she has flown into a passion, and broken out into the "unshackled Doric" of Battersea.[48] They have both got very independent, and say that, in this country, people won't be "hired servants." I shan't miss her much, as I've had to do most things myself lately, and we shall get our washing done by the Chinaman in Moreland for 25s. [shillings] a month. Morris is going on working on the farm at £9 a month, and will board and lodge himself, I shall enjoy the extra work immensely, and shall feel as if I really was living in the Far West, doing everything for myself. Won't it be a blessing never to have the bother of servants?

This whole upset has really been caused by the neighbours, who are so jealous of anyone having servants, as they don't have them themselves; so they have been telling the Morrises that it is *infra dig.* for a white man to be a "hired servant," and how much better they can do on their own account, telling them they ought to have their meals with us and sit in the drawing-room, and so on.[49] Therefore, they have become discontented, ill-tempered, and utterly unbearable.

April 8th. [1885]

We are having a most exciting time of it. The Morrises left on Tuesday. After I had seen them safely off the premises, I saddled up Daisy and rode down towards Three Forks to meet Jem. I rode nearly half way without meeting him; then had to turn back for a new reason, viz. to cook dinner. Just as I got back to town I was hailed by a great big man with a beard, dressed in white leathers and jackboots, so I know he was an Englishman. He exclaimed "How do you do, Mrs. Randall? You do not know me." I recognized the voice, but it was some time before I made out the features of Mr. M—, an old friend, under the disguise of a beard. Then Mr. J—, another Englishman whose acquaintance we had made in the train coming out, came up and shook hands with me.

My first thought was, "Is there enough dinner?" and then I asked them to come down, and here they are now. I get through the work and the cooking well, and give them English dinners every night—soup, meat, and pudding—and then the men all help me to wash up afterwards. Jem, Frank, and I are all pretty busy now, as we have all the domestic duties to perform, besides the boys' ordinary work. We get up at 6 o'clock, Jem lights the fire, whilst I'm dressing, I cook breakfast, which has to be pretty substantial for four hungry men, while Jem and Frank go out and do the stables, milk the cow, &c. Our guests are very good and help too. For breakfast we have porridge (which Americans call "mush"), eggs, fried potatoes, and cold game or meat of some kind, not to mention the "hot biscuits," as they are called out here—breakfast rolls, you would call them; mine, I assure you, are excellent, and the boys seem to think so too.

One afternoon, while Mr. J— and Mr. M— were with us, they said I wanted a holiday; so Frank, who is a capital cook, offered to get dinner ready for us by the time we got back. Accordingly, the rest of us rode off in high glee, and had a jolly cross-country ride, to look at a band of horses which Jem thought would suit Mr. J—, who had come to our country to buy horses. I rode Daisy of course, and Mr. M— rode a half-sister of Daisy's for the first time. He fell in love with her (so did I), and offered Jem £40 for her, which is considered a pretty good price in this country, but Jem says she is worth double that price in the Eastern markets.

When we got back, hungry and happy, about 7 o'clock, we found Frank had a regular banquet ready for us: bean soup, fresh-caught trout, haunch of venison with buffalo-berry jelly, compote of (dried) apples, *and* a beautiful sponge cake, made with nothing but flour, water, sugar, and eggs. When we had done ample justice to his good things we washed up, went into the drawing-room, and, lighting a bright wood fire, the men sat round it, pipe in mouth, in great comfort.

I went to the piano, and soon somebody suggested a song. Mr. J—, who sang very well, gave us "The Place where the Old Horse Died," and he and Mr. M— sang a duet, "Annie Laurie."[50] Frank, after much pressing, sang Besant's rather melancholy ditty out of "Uncle Jack," beginning "The ship was outward bound, when we drank a health around."[51] But Frank's rendering, to a tune of his own, and playing his accompaniment with one finger, was killing. When he came to the line, "One in far Alaska pioneering died," his feelings nearly overcame him, and we thought he wept. Jem gave us the "The Bicester Hunt," and so we went on with song and anecdote til midnight.[52] A thoroughly jolly evening.

Next day the men all rode up to the horse ranche, except Mr. M—, whom I drove in the buggy. The "round-up" was going on, and there were about 300 horses in the corral. You never saw such a scene. Men brandishing clubs, whooping and yelling, more like wild Indians than civilized beings. Horses (they were nearly all wild) rushing from one side of the corral to the other, all huddled together and terrified to death. Well they might be! I'm sure I could not make out what the men wanted them to do, and so I don't see how the poor wretched horses could. Whenever a horse came out of the bunch he was immediately headed back, with shouts, yells, and blows from clubs.

At last, however, I noticed that some were allowed to come by, and were passed through into another corral. Then I found out that they were trying to separate different brands. Each owner has his own brand, and they cut out all belonging to A., branded with a triangle, for instance, and A. takes his horses off; then B. gets his, and so on, until they are all separated. They seem to be very rough, and what with men, and especially boys, wild with excitement, and horses with terror, they make mad work of it.

April 16th. [1885]

Our visitors have just left us, to our great regret, after a jolly visit of a fortnight. We sent them up to the station, with Daisy's half-sister in the buggy [harness] for the first time. She behaved very badly, and one of them had to lead her the whole way. However, she took their things up. The weather was lovely during the whole fortnight, and we were able to sit with our windows open all day. Mr. J—, who is a large cattle-owner, and is therefore not bothered with any small matters like pigs and poultry, observing all the things we have to do now that we have no servants, justly remarked, "Verily it is a life of toil." And so it is; still, we are all very happy, which is the main thing.

I think our visitors enjoyed themselves. Mr. J—, who has not been home for years, said how nice it was to meet a lady again, and sit in an English-looking drawing-room, with some of the refinements of life.[53]

I am wearing summer clothes, and the prairie is green and gorgeous with flowers, especially a little white flower, which grows in bunches and smells delicious.[54] Besides my usual work indoors, I have been painting the garden palings green and washing windows, which latter I find I can do better than I expected.

I'm so thankful to be rid of Mrs. Morris. At all events, I can keep the house clean now, and it is easier to do it myself than it was to make her do it. Jem and Frank say that they live much better, and now we know that every-thing we eat is clean, which is more than we did before. I don't want to be bothered with any more servants if I can possibly manage to do without them; it is no use trying to have them out here; even *good* English ones would be spoilt in a month. The natives are very queer, independent, and rough; it is no use trying to make them into *servants,* and very disagreeable to have half-educated, ill-mannered sort of people to eat and sit with you; and if you had English ones, the natives would soon make them discontented.

I must say one thing. I think the men about here have very good manners, and are always very nice to me. The men who work at the horse ranche all take their hats off to me; not at all because I am the wife of their employer, but because they seem to know that it is good manners to take their hats off to a lady. Jem says they would never dream of taking their hats off to him if I wasn't with him, or showing any other token of respect.

April 25th. [1885]

This last week we have had cold storms of rain and snow; however, we don't mind, as it does so much good to the grass and crops.

Yesterday Jem and I made a great excursion to a ranche about ten miles off to fetch a pig. When we arrived there the man looked at me as I sat in the buggy holding the reins, and said "Won't the woman come in?" Jem smiled, but declined with thanks.

He says that "the woman" is the common term for a man's wife out here. At the same time he says that if he is talking of any female to the natives, and remarks, "What a nice woman Mrs. So-and-so is," they always reply, "Yes, she's a very nice *lady,*" with a great stress on the *lady.*

In a few minutes Jem and the man appeared carrying the pig. We put it in a sack and laid it at our feet, and it took up all the room at the bottom of the buggy. Before we had gone very far I nearly pitched Jem out by driving too fast over a ditch, both his hands being occupied by

Self-portrait of Evelyn Cameron, another English rancher, kneading dough in her kitchen near Terry, Montana, 1904. Isabel Randall's kitchen of twenty years earlier would have been similar. Photograph by Evelyn Cameron. Courtesy the Montana Historical Society, Helena (PAC 90-87.35-5).

holding the pig in. Piggy got his nose out and wanted to bite, uttering the most frightful squeals, which frightened our horse out of his wits. Then down came a frightful storm of wind, rain, and hail. Our hands were nearly frozen, as I had to hold the reins, and Jem the pig. However, after numerous shaves of upsetting the buggy, and determined, but ineffectual, efforts to escape on the part of the pig, we got home safely. Then Jem and I had to lift piggy out bodily, hoist him over some palings, and drop him into the stye. Altogether it was most ludicrous, and, except for the cold and wet, great fun.

I can't tell you what a blessing it is to have got rid of Mrs. Morris. You can't imagine the mess I found every-thing in after she had gone. The house has kept twice as clean ever since. Luckily my men are both very tidy and good about wiping their boots, &c. I generally get through my work at 1 o'clock (breakfasting at 7:15), and have the dinner all ready and half cooked by that time, so that I need not have much to do in the afternoon. There is the kitchen stove to clean; but wood leaves clean ashes.[55] Frank lights the fires for me in the morning. I find I get through my work with very little trouble after all, as I have a certain time fixed for everything, and cook particular things on certain days. I always give them "hot biscuits" for breakfast, fried potatoes, eggs, pork, or bacon, beef, or fish cakes. The cooking I really enjoy, and invent all kinds of new dishes. My sponge cakes rival Frank's for lightness, and I make plenty of pastry and apple tarts.

No fruit is grown in this country at present, so we use "evaporated" or dried fruit, which is cooked like Normandy pippins.[56] The dried fruit, reminds me of the sheep-herder's remark about Montana, when he got up on the 1st of July, to find a snowstorm raging: "Confounded country, where it snows every month of the year, and dried apples are a luxury."

One does feel rather like that one-self, when the weather is bad. There's nothing small about the climate here: when it's good, it's *very* good; and when it's bad, it *is* bad. Luckily the good very much predominates.

We took the washing up to John Chinaman for the first time, this week, and found him doing his hair, which he makes into one long plait, and then coils round his head like a crown.[57] He seemed very good-natured, kept on grinning and saying, "Ah!" "Yah!" but I could not understand a word he said.

May 1st. [1885]

The prairies are simply lovely, quite covered with flowers; pink and white ox-eyed daisys in tiny round bunches, growing quite close to the ground (none of the flowers here have any stalks), yellow flowers (called prickly pear, really a sort of cactus), small pansies, lenten lilies, and many others.[58] The air is literally scented with them all.

We went to Bozeman this week, to buy curtains, carpet, etc., for one of the up-stairs rooms; as a young Englishman is coming out to stay with us. I don't think I ever explained to you how many rooms there are in our house, and what the house is like.

In the first place, there is the new part of the house, two storeys high, consisting of hall, our bed-room and sitting room on each side of the house, immediately behind and joined on to the new part, consisting of three cabins in a row, all joined together, and beyond them a stone dairy. A door opens from the hall into the dining-room, and from the dining-room you go straight through another door into

The remains of Isabel Randall's house, taken from in front of the dairy at the rear. Evidence of the roofline belonging to the original three-room structure she mentions can be seen along the back wall. Photograph by Merrill G. Burlingame, 1933. Courtesy the Gallatin County Historical Society & Pioneer Museum, Bozeman, Montana.

the kitchen (which has another door opening into the garden) and from the kitchen through another door into Jem's den. The up-stairs rooms are plastered and whitewashed; but the drawing-room, our bed-room, the hall, and Jem's den are papered; the dining-room and kitchen walls are boarded and painted. The new two-storey part of the house is built of carefully hewn logs, stained brown, and looks rather nice; the old part is of unhewn logs. The roof is all made of shingles (*i.e.* pieces of wood sawn thin and resembling slates). We have seven good-sized rooms, besides the hall, our small dressing-room and the dairy. They say when this house was built, about fifteen or sixteen years ago, it was *the* show house of the country. Since then, of course, a great many better houses have been built, but ours is very comfortable and quite good enough for this country. I believe it cost the original owner about £500, but we bought the farm, 160 acres, stables, house, and everything as it stood, so it is impossible to say what such a house would cost now. All we've done in the way of building is a new stable, a yard in the shape of a quadrangle, white sheds all round, and the stone dairy, and divers out-houses, pig-styes, chicken-house, &c. From our experience of this, building is still a very expensive amusement, and I think it would always be cheaper to buy a ranche already well improved, than to do any building oneself.

May 16th. [1885]

This week Frank started off to the hills, with a tent and waggon and supplies for a month, to start a new ranche up in the mountains as a summer ranche for our horses. He took another man with him, and we expect he [Frank] will be gone for a month at least. Our English friend also arrived this week, but does not seem to like the life, so I'm afraid he won't stay long with us.

Jem and I went a long ride into the hills north of us, on the other side of the river, to look for a mare and four yearlings, which have strayed off our range. We started at eight, and did not get home until seven. I was rather stiff and tired, but I was riding the laziest horse on the ranche, such a brute, it was almost as hard work to get him along as to walk.

May 31st. [1885]

Last night we were all sitting in Jem's den reading the English papers when I heard Noble (an imported Shire horse) kicking in his box—he has a trick of rolling, and sometimes he gets fast and can't get up—so I told Jem I heard kicking, and, while he was pulling on his boots, I looked out of the window, which faces the stable, and, to my horror, saw the stables in flames![59] We all rushed out at once; but though Jem opened the door of Noble's box and the horse came out, he was either already badly burnt, or suffocated with the smoke; for he only staggered out and immediately fell backwards into the flames and died without a struggle. It was horrible. Noble was such a good horse, and everyone was so fond of him.

The flames spread with frightful rapidity; the buildings being all wood and all in one block, there was no hope of saving anything from the first. We did all we could, getting out saddles, harness and everything we could lay our hands on. Luckily there were no other horses in the stables that night; but one was bad enough, as, apart from our being so fond of him, Noble was worth twenty ordinary horses. The people up in town saw the flames, and came rushing down; but nothing could be done. In half an hour from the time when I first saw the flames, everything was burnt to the ground: all our implements, buggy, and hundreds of odd things were completely destroyed. We were all working hard until two o'clock in the morning, putting out the fire, which had caught dead branches in the trees.

Two cowboys, whom Jem had known for a long time, stayed all night and until quite late the next morning, carrying pails of water to put on the red-hot ashes and smouldering timbers, for fear the wind should get up and blow sparks from them on to the house. It was most fortunate that the wind was not blowing towards the house last night, or *it* must have gone too. Jem and I are still carrying pails of water to put out the ashes; but the danger is over now, I think.

The whole place looks most wretched; all the trees round the house and stables are burnt, and nothing but a heap of ashes and blackened timbers to show where all our beautiful buildings stood. It is most melancholy to see the saddle horses, &c. come trooping up to be fed. They seem quite lost at having no stables to go into, and, of course, there are no oats or hay to feed them with. The chickens, most of which we saved, and pigs, are also wandering around disconsolate; altogether it is most piteous. Of course, we shall have to abandon the idea of our summer ranche in the mountains now, as we must build up this one again.

A few days after the fire, the Amcottses, English people living near here, came over to luncheon. Mrs. Amcotts has just come out from England, and it is so nice to have someone of one's own sex to talk to again.[60] I gave them a grand luncheon, and hope we shall see a great deal of them, as their place is only about fifteen miles from here, just a nice ride to luncheon and back again. Just as they were starting home, Mr. J— turned up again, and stayed a few days with us; of course we were delighted to see him, as he is always so cheery.

June 6th. [1885]

Jem and Frank are hard at work irrigating the crops, wheat and peas. They can't find a man to do it, so they are trying to do it themselves. It seems very interesting work; they fill the different ditches with water, then dam them up at the highest point, cut a hole in one of the banks, and let the water run out on to the land on both sides of the ditch. Nothing will grow out here without irrigation. All this keeps Jem very busy, as he is manager of the Company's horse herd, and has to look after that in addition to his work at home.

Half my time, whilst I'm writing this, is taken up with fighting mosquitoes; they are getting bad now. At night, when we are sitting out in the garden, it is so curious watching the fire-flies flitting in and out of the trees and bushes. The first time I saw them I thought there must be a fire somewhere, and those were the sparks. The nights are getting rather hot now. We generally get up at 4:30 in the morning; I do the house, cooking, &c., and then every day last week I either rode up in the hills with Jem, drove our horses down to the Horse Ranche, or else I rode Daisy, doing errands for Jem.

I went down to the "Pig" Ranche yesterday, and heard that they were thinking of selling their ranche to an Englishman, *and his wife.* So, you see, we shall have quite a colony of English ladies out here soon; however, I can claim the credit of being the pioneer. The principal flowers out now are the wild rose and single sunflower; they grow in profusion.[61]

June 14th. [1885]

I've been having a pretty lively week of it. Jem started for Helena on Monday, eighty miles, on horseback, and isn't back yet. I haven't heard anything about him, though I expected him back yesterday. He went to buy a horse to replace poor old Noble. Frank also went on Monday to hunt horses, and I'm all alone in my glory; not quite though, as we have a young Englishman, fresh from the old country, staying with us.

On Tuesday morning, the latter wanted to go to the "Pig" Ranche to borrow some tennis balls, so I saddled and bridled my little "cayuse" (or cow pony) which I always keep picketed, and started out with a huge long whip (our gentle mares are such wretches, they stand still and kick at you instead of going on, when you want to drive them anywhere; so you have to use a whip) to find our horses. After plunging through swamp and brush for some time, I found them all, drove them home and corralled them all by myself. Then I caught our friend's horse, saddled and bridled it for him, and having walked a quarter of a mile to open a gate for him, I went home to enjoy my own company for the day.

He came back in the evening, bringing the balls, and we had some grand games of tennis. We had rolled a place up on the flat; it was pretty rough and uneven, but good enough for us to enjoy playing. We cut two poles from a tree, and stuck up some wire netting, and marked out the ground with whitewash; unfortunately, we didn't get the corners quite square, but it didn't matter much. Harry (Jem's cousin) came down, and I got him to stay the night.[62] Next day Mr. H—, another Englishman, appeared, directly after breakfast, and when I had done my work, we played tennis all day.

Suddenly we saw someone else coming, and lo and behold! it was Mr. Morris turned up again! He only stayed one day, being on his way to England. I must say I envied him. Frank came back last night, not having found the horse which he went to look for. To-day we all spent in making a fence to keep pigs off the peas. Before he had finished breakfast, down came Mr H— to see us. He told me a lot of news. People do gossip out here, *and* quarrel.

There were "six-shooters" out up at the Hotel the other evening—a terrible row going on; of course everyone had been drinking this disgusting whiskey. It's rather exciting hearing about it afterwards, but they say whiskey is the curse of this country.

Frank and I were playing tennis yesterday, when the man, who is hauling lumber for our new stables, came by. He stopped and gazed, then said, "Having a game of ball?" He grinned and seemed to think it a great joke. When we had finished, we met him coming back, and he said to Frank, "I guess you let the lady win." He wanted to know if it was an amusement. They are funny people. We've got a man working for us now, who is a tremendous talker; since Jem has been away, whenever I show my nose anywhere near him, he calls out, "Say Mrs.", and then asks me my opinion about the stables, &c., and boasts of what a splendid building he is going to make. I must tell you that all the natives think that our tennis ground is the ground plan for our new stables. The white lines puzzled them exceedingly, but that is the solution they always arrive at. Oh! the people here have a high opinion of themselves, and tell pretty good yarns; one never believes more than a quarter of what they say.

I'm sorry to say that the woman, who used to come once a week to scrub floors, can't come any more, so I shall have to learn. I daresay it isn't so hard as it looks. I wish one or two of the girls I know, who complain of having nothing to do at home, would come out here. They would find plenty to do, and amusement too.[63]

June 23rd. [1885]

Jem came back last Tuesday, having been away over a week. He brought back a beautiful big black horse, but not so good a horse as Noble, we think, though everyone else is in raptures about him. Jem bought a band of mares when he was away, and stopped the night at the Amcottses, next day there was a regular procession, Jem leading his big horse in front, then a band of about twenty mares and colts, and then Mrs. Amcotts and her brother driving them. They lunched here, and rode home in the evening.

One day last week we took a holiday, and rode down to spend the day with them. It was very hot riding, and in some places the mosquitoes were terrible. They literally covered our horses, until we could hardly see what colour they were. I am getting nearly devoured, but I console myself by thinking that next year I shan't mind these pests. They always bite people worse the first year. We had a very jolly day with the Amcottses and got back here at 11 P.M. It was deliciously cool riding back in the evening. Major Amcotts congratulated me on having a holland habit, and thought it looked so cool.[64] I never wear a habit at all about home, neither does Mrs. Amcotts.

I was left all alone the other day, as Jem and Frank were both hunting horses a long way off, in different directions. When it began to get dark, I shut all the doors, put chairs against them, and then departed to bed. Luckily I never think of robbers out here, so I was quite happy. I woke up in the middle of the night, hearing Jem coming down the hill, singing "Some Day" to let me know who it was, so that I mightn't be alarmed. It was just one o'clock, and he had ridden, I don't know how many miles, so as not to leave me alone.

Our new stables are being put up. They are much smaller than the old ones, but we hope to improve them some day. My bread has just risen, so I must finish this and attend to it. I not only have to make my own bread out here, but my own yeast, which is made with potatoes and hops, and old yeast to make it ferment. I have to make it very often in summer, as it soon goes sour.

July 12th. [1885]

It is getting dreadfully hot now. They say July and August are the two hottest months in the year, just as January and February are the coldest. There are thunder-storms nearly every afternoon. They are much more violent here than they are in England, but then everything in this country is on a large scale. I am getting [to be] quite a useful hand on the ranche. I have ridden out alone in the hills several times this week, *I do like it so.* It is so nice to ride to all the different bunches of horses which I see in the distance studying the brands, and then, when I come to those I want, cutting them out, and driving them down to the ranche. The horse I ride seems to enjoy the whole thing too. I use a cow-pony for this work, as Daisy is too excitable. My being able to do all this, saves Jem a lot of time, as he and Frank are very busy just now farming and irrigating.

We had hired a man to work by the month at £9 a month to do this; but when our stables and everything were burnt, we set him to build a new stable. He got so elated with his skill as a carpenter, that he went up to town one day and said "it wasn't likely that a first-rate *mechanic* was going to work for only £9 a month!" He never came to work any more, and it was only by accident that we learned the reason. He never told us he was going to leave, but quietly left us in the lurch, just at the busy time, when it is quite impossible to find anyone else; so the boys made up their minds to turn farm-hands themselves. Though they are quite at home when it comes to handling stock, I don't know what kind of farmers they'll make. I think gentlemen generally make better stockmen than farm-hands, but, of course, out here men have to do anything that turns up.

On Thursday, after I had done my work, I started off at 8 o'clock to Three Forks, riding Daisy, and leading another horse. I had to go slowly all the way, as the other horse led so badly and kept pulling back, which nearly drove Daisy frantic, and started her "bucking" a little. However, I managed to stick on her and not let the other horse go. I lunched with the Amcottses, and saw all the other English people down there. Soon after I had started home a terrific thunder-storm came on. Luckily there was a ranche about a mile farther on (American), so I galloped on there as fast as I could, jumped the fence in front of the house, to the great astonishment of the natives, and asked for shelter. I stayed there chatting until the storm was over. The people were very pleasant. But the house! You can't imagine anything dirtier—only two rooms in it. The room we sat in had no carpet and *such* a dirty floor; no furniture except a deal table, two wooden chairs, and a rough bunk covered with blankets, which answered the purpose of a sofa by day and bed by night.[65] There was nothing like the comfort which you would see in a farm-labourer's cottage at home, and yet these people were well off.

When the storm was over, I trotted on, but had not gone far when down came the rain in sheets, so I galloped about three miles further, and got to the Pig Ranche, went in there, and found the owners at home. They luckily had a fire in the kitchen, so I dried my dripping garments and helped them to cook supper, which I afterwards also helped them to eat. Then I rode home in the dark, and found the boys quietly smoking in front of the house, imagining that I was safely at Three Forks.

The Amcottses came over on Saturday to stay the night, and we had a very jolly evening, songs and music. Mrs. Amcotts made such a pretty sketch of the house, which I will send you. We are going to try and get a holiday soon, and hope to start on my birthday. We are going up into the mountains, and shall take all our gentle mares and colts up with us. Then we can leave home happily knowing that they won't be stolen in our absence. The boys hope to have done irrigating, and won't have much to do until the crops are cut. I saw Harry [Lowndes] up in town today, and he looked so miserably ill, that I asked him to come down and rest until he was well. He has got a touch of mountain fever.

July 28th. [1885]

We have been busy haymaking all this week. It is a very nice job here, as it is cut, and raked up into rows, cocked (with the horse-rake) and carried all in the same day. I drove the hay-rake all one day. It was quite a luxury driving, sitting on a high spring-seat, and pulling up and letting down the lever constituted carriage exercise. Perhaps if people tried horse-raking when they are ordered carriage exercise, they would get a little of the latter. We have done all our hay without any help, only Jem and Frank and myself. Jem has just been in to say that if I can come now he will help me pick peas, so a good offer must not be refused. We have about twenty acres of peas to feed the pigs in winter. At present we are the pigs, as we live on green peas, fish, eggs, and milk. Meat won't keep a day in this weather; besides, it's too hot to eat meat. The shooting season begins on August 1st, so we shall get plenty of game then.

August 2nd. [1885]

I am writing from Three Forks: Jem had to drive a bunch of horses to a ranche near here, so I came to help him, and we stopped the night with the Amcottses. We are going home at 4 o'clock in the morning, so as to ride while it is cool. The heat has been awful all this week; the thermometer has been up to 109 in the shade, and never lower than 96. What it must have been in the sun I don't know. Frank was quite knocked up by it one morning, and had to come in and lie down, and Jem was as bad another day. I haven't felt it yet quite so bad, though I've been riding in the sun most days.

On Tuesday we hope to be off to the mountains for a week's holiday, taking our waggon, tent, and camp outfit. It will be delicious to get up to the mountains, where it is cool, and do nothing but shoot and fish and lie about in the shade. I am to have a complete holiday, as Frank has promised to do the cooking, and there will be no house to clean. It will really seem, too, as if one was out in a wild country.

August 19th. [1885]

I could not write last Sunday, as we were in camp up in the mountains. We started on Thursday, driving about forty head of horses with us. Jem and I rode and drove the horses and Frank went on in front with the waggon, taking the tent, canteen, and ammunition. The first day we went about twenty miles, and camped by a spring of delicious cold water.[66]

It was so jolly camping out. Frank made a fire on the ground, and cooked frying-pan bread, made of flour, water, and baking-powder. You fill the frying pan with dough, put it on the fire until the bottom is done, and then toss it in the air to turn it and bake the other side. It isn't half bad bread. We had bacon, eggs, and coffee for supper. It all tasted so good after our ride. It was perfectly delicious at night sitting round the camp-fire, breathing the beautiful fresh air, scented with the perfumed smoke from the logs of smouldering cedar, and looking up at the clear sky, studded with millions of stars, flashing in all their glory; not a sound to be heard except what was made by our horses busily cropping the short sweet grass, or the murmuring of our voices, softened by the pleasing languor of a light fatigue, disturbed now and then by the melancholy howl of a distant coyote. So we sat and talked of everything under the sun, until at last we got to hunting and a comparison between the delights of the chase at home and abroad, and I think our vote was in favour of the former, bigoted Britons that we are. Then someone asked Jem about that story of the bear and the fusee.[67]

"That reminds me," said Jem, "smoking saved that hero's life; so I'll light my pipe in grateful memory."

Suiting the action to the word, he took an ember from the fire, puffed volumes of smoke for a few minutes, and began.

"You recollect Jack B—. Well, though there *is* a temptation to some minds to draw the long bow with regard to snakes and bears, yet I don't think that Jack was given that way, and I believe that his story, though strange, was true.[68]

"It seems he was hunting down in Wyoming some-where, and desperate keen on bears. So one fine morning he dropped on to an old she-bear with cubs—not exactly the most amiable creature to meet at the best of times. However, Jack didn't often miss; so, after a quick look for a handy tree in case of accidents, up went the express. The crack of the rifle produced a yell from Madame Bruin, but no other result, except a very lively movement in the direction of Master Jack, who, on his side, made an equally lively one in the direction of the tree, which he gained with very little to spare, and a very creeply feeling about his extremities, as he dragged himself into a place of safety, minus his gun.

"'Here's a go!' communed our friend. 'I'm up a tree with a vengeance, and, to make matters worse, a raging she-bear underneath. Well, I believe I'll take a smoke, and look this business square in the eye.'

"Accordingly he filled his pipe, and struck a fusee to light it. Just for fun, he dropped the fusee on Madame Bruin's back. As soon as it burnt through the hair, she jumped as if she was shot, then she rolled and growled, and bit at her back, and went on like a mad thing, until the match cooled down, when she returned to the tree, foaming at the mouth, her eyes like hot coals, and began tearing at the tree, while making violent endeavours to get on level terms with her persecutor. A few more fusees deftly dropped at intervals only served to make her madder and madder; and Jack's face grew longer and longer. He began to think which was the stronger feeling in a bear, rage or hunger, and hoped it was the latter.

"Just then the bear came open-mouthed at him, and, standing on her hind legs did her level best to reach him, into the red mouth of the bear dropped a red-hot fusee. Jack said her face was a picture. She halloa'ed, she rolled, she foamed, and at last she ran; just as hard as legs could carry her, she scuttled off into the brush. Jack's medicine had settled her.

"So you see," said Jem, knocking the ashes out of his pipe, "there's some good in smoking, after all, and I'll smoke another pipe on the strength of it. A pipe never does go so well as round a camp-fire. Throw another log on, Frank, like a good fellow, and we'll smoke one more pipe and turn in. By-the-bye, did I ever tell you about Colonel H— and his patent cartridges? They must have been some left over from a Government contract, but no matter. He was hunting bear somewhere near Clark's Fork, I think, and one day he tracked a bear for a good while, and, just as he caught sight of the critter, he disappeared into a cave.[69]

"The Colonel didn't like to be beat. It was bear he was hunting, and bear he wanted; so up he went to the cave, down he went on his hands and knees, and looked in. First of all he couldn't see a thing. At last he saw something like two red-hot coals.

"'Ah!' thinks the Colonel, 'I've got you; but if I don't shoot straight, you'll get me. You've backed into the cave, and you can't get any further in, and you can't get out, unless I do. Well, here goes.'

"He drew a bead on that bear, and aimed steady and true right between the red-hot coals, pulled the trigger, and—click!

"'Missed fire, by Jove!'

"He kept his eye on those two red-hot coals, and they got bigger. He didn't dare to move, he didn't dare to breathe. He had one barrel left, and he thought he would keep that until the hot coals grew larger; if he missed this time, he was done. It wasn't altogether nice, but he waited. At last the hot coals stopped.

"'Now is my chance,' says the Colonel; and he took a long, steady aim.

"Click! Missed fire again. The Colonel said, when he heard that 'click,' he thought he could feel for a man on trial for his life, when the jury says 'Guilty.' He didn't move a muscle, but kept his eyes on the red-hot coals. Bigger and bigger they grew; nearer and nearer they came; and he thought it was all over. At last they stopped. He supposed they were stationary for a few seconds, but it seemed to him as if it was for hours. Then they moved, Thank heaven! they grew less; he breathed again. They disappeared altogether; still he dared not move. He knelt there motionless, it seemed to him, for hours.

"At last he thought he'd chance it; he could not stay there for ever. So he got up, and moved cautiously backwards, with his eye on the cave, and Bruin gone. You bet, there wasn't a happier man in Wyoming that minute than Colonel H—. He went back to camp, opened his cartridges, and they were loaded—with sawdust! He opened the whole lot, and found the same harmless material in them all. He concluded to load his own cartridges for the future. These he had bought ready loaded in New York."

"That will do," says Frank, "give him the kettle."[70]

But this was a true bill all the same.

"Well," says Jem, "You are getting sceptical; let's turn in, or I shall be spinning you bear stories until daylight."

In a few minutes we were sleeping the sleep of the weary, as if there wasn't such a thing as a rattle-snake in the world. We heard afterwards, that a man camping here a few weeks before had killed five of those charming creatures on this very spot.

Next morning, as we were boiling coffee, watching some grouse frying, and warming our hands over the camp-fire, we saw a man come riding into camp with something behind his saddle. Deer would not be in season for about a week; but deer it was. Jem and Frank began chaffing the hunter about killing deer out of season.

"Well," he said, "you see, I ran across this blessed critter, and was so close to him that he got scared, didn't look where he was going, ran his head against a rock, and broke his neck; so I had to bring him along, you see."

"I was just going to exclaim, "What an extra-ordinary thing," when I observed a sly twinkle in Frank's eye, and desisted.

"Had any more of that kind of luck?" said Frank.

"Well, no, not exactly, but one did attack me the other day, and I had to kill him in self-defense. They are dangerous at times."

As accidents will happen and a man must defend his life when attacked, we didn't refuse a shoulder of venison, in return for our grouse and coffee, even though deer *were* out of season.

After breakfast we packed up the camp outfit, started off again, and did twenty miles leisurely, and got into camp about four o'clock. We picketed two horses, pitched our tent, cooked supper, and, after a careful search for rattle-snakes turned in. Our drive took us up and down some frightful places, as we camped high up in the mountains, at least 6,000 feet above the level of the sea.

The country was perfectly lovely up there, just under the timber line, and the grass was up to our horses' knees. The scenery was something wonderful. Rough broken hills, deep gorges with both sides clothed with a thick growth of quaking ash making a lovely tender green, in startling contrast to the bright yellow of the bunch grass.[71] Foaming streams of water rushing down the gorges, and up and beyond, the dark masses of pine, reaching up to the mountain tops, capped with glistening white snow, and over and above all, the glorious canopy of the bright blue sky. There is certainly a wonderful brightness of colour in this whole country, when it is flooded, as it usually is, with the sunshine; and something exhilarating about it, which defies depression of spirits and makes one feel light-hearted and joyous as a child. It was delicious to jump up at daybreak, and a whole day of delight before us. For it *is* a pleasure to spend a whole day riding over your free grouse moor or deer forest, with the certainty of a good day's sport amongst grouse and prairie chicken, and a possibility of a white and black tail deer, bear, or even the monarch of these mountains, the mighty Wapiti itself.[72] There is pleasure too in sitting round the camp-fire in the chilly mornings, warming your hands and cooking breakfast, which you are more than ready for, with the appetite acquired from mountain air and a good conscience. To feel that you are safe for that day, at least, from bad news or any of the toils and troubles of this work-a-day world. Then, breakfast over, to put a frugal lunch in your pocket, mount your horse and away, to wander at your own sweet will (with no one to say you "nay") over your vast hunting ground.

When we struck game of any sort, the boys would tumble off their horses, and leave me to catch them as best I could, while they hit or missed, as the case might be. Another time we would picket our horses and go afoot, through bunch-grass knee high, or make our way as best we could, through the dense groves of brush and quaking ash. Following Jem through one of these, I saw him stop suddenly and beckon to me; there, not two yards in front of him, was an immense rattle-snake, with its head up ready to strike, and rattling with all its might.[73] Such a wicked sound and evil-looking brute. We watched it for some seconds, until Jem put up his gun and blew its head off. It was the first one I had seen, and I never wish to see another. It had ten rattles and was very nearly four feet long. Another step or two, and Jem must have trodden on it, and there would not have been much chance for a man to recover from a bite up there, miles away from remedies.

Then towards evening we would make our way back to camp, laden with feathered game and a settled conviction that, to-morrow at any rate, we should kill a deer, as we had found plenty of tracks that day. So presently we would get into camp, light the fire, cook supper, and then sit round the blazing logs, pleasantly tired, and chat until some one proposed turning in. There is a wonderful charm about this sort of gipsy life, and it is the most perfect rest.

However, our holiday was cut short, and not in the pleasantest way. I got a kind of sunstroke, and was rather bad all night and the next day; so Jem thought it best to break up our camp and go home. We started early and went right through in one day, reaching home about 11 P.M. We got off the trail in the dark and had to get out and grope with our hands for the ruts. Luckily there were no prickly pears or rattle-snakes about.

We got home Thursday and the Amcottses and Mr. H— were coming to us on Saturday, to stay until Monday. The amount of dust that had accumulated in our absense was fearful, and I was in despair of ever getting the house cleaned and tidied in time. However, Jem put in a whole day helping me, and by Saturday evening I felt I could receive my guests with an easy conscience. Even out here, you see, a woman can't forget her instincts, and anything like dust and dirt is an abhorence.

Our guests arrived about 6 o'clock in the evening, and, while Jem was helping them to make their horses comfortable, Frank and I were busy in the kitchen; we had arranged flowers on the table in the morning, and, with a snowy tablecloth and bright silver, I thought our dinner-table looked quite gay. We had a delightful evening and were all very jolly. These little gatherings are very enjoyable to us exiles, and give one a taste of what this country might be, if it were settled more thickly with English people.

Whilst the Amcottses were with us, we had a sort of tea picnic, which was rather fun. The others had been fishing all day (I have not been able to go out in the sun, since I was ill in the mountains), so, at about 5 o'clock, I put Jem's saddle on a very sedate old mare, and sallied out to find them, laden with a basket well stocked with tea, cake, &c. I needn't say my arrival was hailed with acclamation, and we all fell to in high glee. The fish ought to have been grateful to me, as, after tea, the men declared they had caught fish enough (in fact, there was a noble heap of slain on the grass), and voted in favour of sitting under the trees to smoke and chat; so there we sat, talking about "the old countrie" until our duties summoned us home. To-morrow we begin harvest, so there won't be much leisure until it is over.

You ask me about vegetables. This year was not a great success. It's true we had plenty of peas and some spinach and turnips, and we have a grand crop of potatoes; but we did not irrigate enough, so the things got dried up at a critical time and never really recovered from it. Next year we hope to do much better, as we know more about it. I must go and see about my cooking now, so I must close this.

You wonder that I have time to write, when I have so much to do; I confess that it does seem a good deal to do, but it is wonderful how much one can do with a little method; and every day it becomes easier as I get more accustomed to doing everything. It makes one think how little servants must do at home. Here am I, cook, parlour-maid, house-maid, and scullery-maid all rolled into one; and I declare, as long as one's health is good, I would much sooner do it all myself than be bothered with servants; out here, at any rate. In spite of all my work, I have plenty of time to amuse myself, which the American women never seem to do, for they spend the whole time indoors.

August 30th. [1885]

Since my last letter, I have actually been to a ball! We drove down to Three Forks to stay with the B—'s for the event. They are English people, consisting of a young married couple, her father, sister, and brother; so they make quite an addition to our English society.

To return to the ball. It began about 8 o'clock, and was held in the dining-room of the hotel. I wore my red day dress, as Mrs. B— told me no one wore evening dresses. When we arrived we found the room full of people, and the women dressed up in all sorts of costumes—the belles of the ball, two sisters, in red cotton-backed satin skirts and curtain-muslin tops—and the men, some in black coats, some in brown coats, and some in no coats at all. Such a queer-looking lot!

We had made up our minds only to dance amongst ourselves, and as we were a party of ten or twelve, we could manage very well. The *band* consisted of a fiddle and a banjo, and played the same tune all the way through. The players sat on a raised platform, and on the same place stood a little man, looking full of importance, in dress clothes and white kid gloves, waving a stick. He proved to be the master of ceremonies.

"Every man has a number marked on his ticket, from one to thirty-six, or whatever the number of men may be. Only the men pay for tickets, and invite the ladies."

I soon discovered the reason of the numbered tickets, for presently the M.C. called out "One, five, eight, ten," and so on—naming about sixteen numbers—"will dance the next dance.[74] Get your partners."

You see there are many more men than women, so the M.C. calls out who are to dance so as to give all the men an equal chance of dancing (liberty, equality, fraternity!); otherwise only a favoured few would get any dancing, and all the rest would be left out in the cold. Then the sets were formed, and, to my great surprise, the M.C. called out what they were going to do in each figure—for instance, "Swing your partners twice to the right, and return to your places." "Advance and retire twice, swing your partners to the right, and return to your places." Every now and then he uttered a strange yell, which I thought must be and old Indian battle-cry, sounding like "Elemengo," but this, being interpreted, was French (?) "A la main gauche."

Most of the dances were squares, but they had a few waltzes. These were beautifully danced, though very slowly. I never saw better dancing, the only peculiarity being that the men put both hands round the girl's waist, clasping them behind, first of all carefully spreading a silk handkerchief on her back to prevent his hands soiling her dress. A most delicate and certainly necessary attention, as the men wore no gloves. The girl put one hand on each of her partner's shoulders. At the end of each dance the M.C. sung out "all promenade." Whereupon they all marched round the room arm-in-arm, generally in solemn silence. In fact, from the absence of conversation and the solemnity of their faces, you might have imagined that they were performing a religious ceremony. Do not the English, but also all English-speaking nations, take their pleasure sadly? Certainly these people do, as regards dancing, at any rate.

About 12 o'clock they trooped off to supper. We waited until they were all settled, and then we went down and found a capital supper—chicken, chicken salad, several kinds of cakes, coffee and tea. All this was nicely cooked by a Chinaman. About 1 o'clock the scene began to get rather animated, some of the men beginning actually to talk and even to shout. An Englishman whispered to me "Whisky," and advised us to beat a retreat, as, he said, these dances generally degenerated into a bear fight, and frequently a man fight, towards morning; so we quietly departed, rather pleasantly surprised at a ball in the Rockies.

The natives are passionately fond of dancing, and think nothing of driving thirty or forty miles to a ball. They kept this one up until 7 o'clock in the morning. Girls are certainly favoured out here—not the smallest chance of posing as a wallflower; and in the more important matter of choosing partners for life, it is literally only a case of choice, as the men outnumber the women ten to one. Matrimony, like death, spares neither age nor condition. I have seen young girls of thirteen and hideous old girls of fifty snapped up eagerly as soon as they arrived in the country, which reminds me of the advice given by an old lady, to a young wife going out to the Colonies, and looking out for a maid to accompany her. "Take a pretty one my dear," said the old lady, "for, ugly or pretty, she will have an offer of marriage before she has been out a week; and while your ugly girl will say 'Yes' to the first offer she gets and leave you, your pretty one will be harder to please, and will say 'No' several times before she consents."

Marriages are very simple affairs out here. They are generally performed by a Justice of the Peace, *not* assisted by any representative of any church, and in strict privacy. One couple we know (all this, of course, refers only to natives) were actually married on the open prairie, sitting in their waggon, while the J.P. sat in his buggy! A funeral is a much grander affair. All the neighbours turn out in waggons, buggies, and saddle-horses, to follow a corpse to the grave, in a long and melancholy procession. The other day a deputation waited on Jem to ask if the Company (of which he is manager, and which owns most of the land round here) would give a piece of land for a cemetery.

One of the deputation suggested a certain hill, because "they would be nice and dry up there." On Jem saying he would consider the matter, one man said, "Well, I guess you must be quick because old man Morrison's woman is dying; she can't last more than a week, and he wants to be sure of a place to put her."[75]

September 6th. [1885]

I'm so delighted that there is a chance of Godfrey coming out here.[76] He might come out here next spring, and stay with us six months, to see if he liked the country and life, and then go home for the winter before settling down here for good. Jem says that is the only thing to do; that it is quite impossible to say whether anyone will like the life and get on, or to say what they had better do. He says he thinks there are plenty of good openings here, but everything depends upon the man himself.

Of course Godfrey could not do any hard work, and there would be no occasion for him to do any. No one does except "grangers," for I don't call riding after stock "hard work." Of course it is, really, but still it is very different to the regular manual "grind" of a farm-hand. I don't think *gentlemen* are fitted for that. Jem and Frank have tried it this summer, just to show they could do it in a pinch, but it has nearly killed them, working so hard at things that they are not accustomed to in this frightful heat. They both say they will never try it again.

I think gentlemen are inclined to work too hard for the first few hours, and are then utterly exhausted and dead for the remainder of the day, and yet feel obliged to go on to the end. They can't work steadily and quietly like a working man who has been used to it all his life. It is just like putting a high-mettled, well-bred horse to plough with a cold-blooded cart-horse. The thoroughbred wears himself out by trying to do too much at first, whereas the cart-horse goes steadily lugging all day without exciting himself. Jem says that he thinks an Englishman, who has been used to hunting in England and ridden all his life, can kill a Western American when it comes to riding, and that he can ride greater distances with greater ease to himself and the horse he is on; and that stockwork is all that an Englishman is good for, if he wants to go in for hard work, though, of course, it is useful for him to know how to do all kinds of ordinary farm-work.

They call the farmers here "grangers," as distinct from ranch-men or stock-men, and it is rather a term of reproach—not quite that, either—but still the granger is held in low estimation by the stock-man. In Montana the latter is king, and all the laws seem framed to his advantage and to the disadvantage of the granger.

The term "ranche" really means the same as the English word "farm". I used to think that a ranche consisted of thousands of acres, like the Australian "run"; but now I find that a little farm of even forty acres, with a one-roomed log cabin, is a "ranche," and what we call the "range" answers to the Australian "run," with this difference, that whereas the Australian pays rent for or owns his "run," and has it all to himself, fenced in, the Western stock-man has his range free, but his stock run in common with several other peoples', and are not fenced in except by the natural boundaries of the range, such as rivers or chains of mountains. Thus our range extends over some three or four hundred thousand acres, and is bounded on three sides by rivers and one side by a chain of high mountains.

The cowboy on his hardy pony is the Western rancher's wire fence, and it is his duty to see that no stock strays outside the natural boundaries of the range, and to bring back any that do. There are lots of horses which we don't see more than once a year, but we don't feel uneasy about them, as if they should stray off the range we should probably hear of them. Of course stock men lose some by straying every year, but the loss sustained is a very small rent to pay for the enormous amount of land on which the stock run.

If Godfrey comes out here only for his health, he could not come to a better country. People from the Eastern States, suffering from chest complaints, come here and get quite well and strong. The Morrises were an example of this. Their horrid coughs got less and less all last winter, even in the very cold weather, and finally vanished altogether. They said they were never free from a cough in England.[77] Then Godfrey could ride, shoot, and fish to his heart's content. I have been fishing every day this week, and kept the larder well supplied, as the boys have been too busy harvesting to have time for shooting or fishing. Jem gave me a new fishing rod.

I was out on the range hunting horses yesterday, found what I wanted and drove them in all by myself, feeling very proud of my performance. Jem says I shall soon make a first-rate cowboy. I tried my hand with the lasso one day and caught a little colt, as he ran by, at the first attempt, but would not spoil it by trying again; so I looked very grand and said "I wondered that men ever missed, and that I knew it was quite easy, though they did make such a fuss about it."

Frank has just been out shooting, as the rain stopped their work, and brought in any amount of teal and duck, enough to last a week. I have learnt to salt fish, so that they will keep good for a week or ten days. We are all going down to stay with Mr. H— for two nights next week. Mr. H— and Harry [Lowndes] were staying with us this week.

September 20th. [1885]

Such a letter from a dear friend in England this week! "How can I do such dreadful things? Camping out amongst rattle-snakes! getting sunstrokes! driving wild horses! and, as if these out-of-door terrors weren't bad enough, working like a slave indoors and killing myself with hard work."

Does it sound so appalling? Well, it never struck me as being anything out of the way at the time. But, of course, things out here *appear* worse to people at home than they really are.

Now for the reverse side of the medal. I pass over the rattle-snakes. Sunstroke—now you might get that in England—and, then, I only mentioned it to show how hot it is, for you know I always rather boasted of being able to stand extremes of heat and cold. Driving wild horses! Well, perhaps that *sounds* appalling; but it doesn't mean driving them in harness, but riding another horse behind them and driving them, like you see in an old man driving up the milk cows at home, only the old man is on foot and the cows don't go out of a walk.

Now for the other indictment—indoors. Now I like the work. When you have no society, and everyone is *out of doors* working, you *must* work for amusement *indoors.* I do think this is the best sort of life. One feels so much better and happier; and so would any other healthy girl. Of course, washing dishes, scrubbing floors, and all the rest of it, does sound and seem a great hardship to people at home; but I can assure you it doesn't seem so when you do it. I know I would not exchange my happy, free, busy, healthy life out here, for the weariness and *ennui* that makes so many girls at home miserable. I don't feel myself to be an object of pity—quite the reverse; I only wonder that more people who are miserable on small incomes at home, don't come out here and be happy. What is poverty at home would be riches out here, and one doesn't have to spend half one's income in keeping up appearances; and there's the glorious health everyone enjoys in this country. How many thousands a year is that worth?

No! I think people out here, with moderate means, are infinitely happier than people in the same condition at home. What do you gain by being out here? Health and happiness, plenty to do, plenty of interests and amusements. Indoors you can have your piano, all the newest books at a fraction of the price you have to pay at home (I am reading the latest three-volume novel, which costs a guinea at home, and costs me a shilling here), all the periodicals and English papers—a little late, perhaps, but what does that matter?—and you can see a fellow-mortal now and then to discuss them all with. Out of doors you have your horses, your grouse-moor, deer-forests, and all free. Let us see what you lose. Society, and the luxury of sitting with your hands folded, seeing others do badly what you feel you can do much better yourself. As a drawback even to this latter luxury, you have the endless bother of servants, and as for Society, we shall get that by degrees. You will say, "All very well while you're young." Granted; and when we are old it will be time enough "to creep home, and take our place there, the sick and old among." Meanwhile I am thoroughly happy with my varied occupations and amusements, and if I have some cares (and who has not?), have I not many joys to counter-balance them; so give me my home in

> The West, the West, the land of the free,
> Where the mighty Missouri rolls down to the sea,

and I am more than content.[78]

September 26th. [1885]

Last week I spent two or three days with the B—s, and left Jem alone in his glory, as Frank was away. Having cooked enough to last until I came back, I put on a clean frock, climbed up into the buggy, and drove off, enjoying my drive immensely.

Perhaps I shouldn't have enjoyed it quite so much, if I had known that the Helena coach was stopped the other day by highwaymen, or "road agents," as they are called. No one was hurt, however, or robbed, as one of the "road agents" had warned the proprietors, and agreed to help to capture his accomplice when the attempt was made, which he did successfully; and this Western Dick Turpin is now cooling his heels in jail. Highway robbers, or "road agents," are scarce now, though some years ago they were as plentiful as blackberries. I heard such a capital story of the presence of mind of a lady on one occasion, when a coach was stopped, that I must tell you.

She was travelling by coach (before the days of railroads) to join her husband, a distance of some hundred miles. On the journey one of her fellow-passengers said to her:

"I have got about a thousand dollars in my pocket-book, and feel rather uneasy about road agents. Would you mind concealing it in your dress, and giving it to me at the end of the journey? If we are stopped, they are less likely to search you than me."

She complied with his request, and accordingly hid the money in her dress. Towards evening there was a shout of "Throw up your hands!" and four men on horseback, with masked faces, appeared in the road, pointing their pistols at the driver, who promptly pulled up.

Two men then appeared at the side of the coach, and ordered the passengers to give up their arms, which they did. The robbers then ordered them to "shell out." Our friend of the morning gave up a few dollars, and was congratulating himself on the success of this precaution, when, to his horror, the lady said in a clear voice:

"I have got a thousand dollars, but I suppose I must give them up," producing at the same time our friend's hardly-earned roll of "greenbacks" from the folds of her dress."

He looked unutterable things. The robbers then rifled the treasure-box, and rode off delighted with their booty.

As soon as they were gone, our friend began abusing the lady in no measured terms, accusing her of having betrayed him, and given up all he had in the world, out of sheer fright. She only replied oracularly that "he would see," and that she could give no explanation now.

When she got to the end of her journey, she asked him to come and stay the night at her house, adding that her husband would be very glad to see him. To this he assented, saying, in an injured tone of voice, that it was the least she could do, seeing that through her treachery he was without a cent in the world. He was royally entertained, his hostess exerting herself to amuse him; but not a word of explanation was vouchsafed by either host or hostess, and he went to bed in no very enviable state of mind.

On entering the dining-room in the morning, he was met by his host, who said:

"Here are your thousand dollars, which my wife ventured to borrow in case of emergency. The fact was she had twenty thousand dollars, which she was bringing to me, concealed in her dress, and she thought that by giving up at once the thousand dollars entrusted to her by you she would disarm suspicion, and save any further search on the part of the robbers. Her quickness, as you know now, saved me from a heavy loss."[79]

Our friend apologized for his unfounded suspicion and rudeness of the previous day; and breakfast, no doubt, proved a far cheerier meal than the supper of the night before.

I spent two days with the B—'s and enjoyed myself very much. They have got a piano, and are all musical; some young Englishmen came to supper one night, who all sang very well; so we had plenty of singing, and, as a wind up, a miniature dance. I say "miniature," because the room was only large enough for one couple at a time; I brought Mrs. B— home with me to stay a few days, to have a little rest, which she much needed. She stayed with us about a week, and, when my work was done, I drove her about in the buggy; we went on some most beautiful drives, either up in the mountains or down by the river.

The autumn tints are beginning, the cottonwood leaves turn such gorgeous yellows and reds, and, mixed with the green of the cedar, the colorings are perfectly grand.

Yesterday Jem and I drove to Bozeman to do some shopping; started at half-past seven, crossed one river and several creeks, and got into town at half-past eleven. It was eighteen miles of an abominable road full of great round stones; the smallest as big as a cricket-ball and some a good deal bigger than a man's head, and then, when we got within five miles of Bozeman, and amongst the settlements, we got into lanes, *i.e.* where the road is fenced on both sides. Here the soil was a rich black loam, and very wet, and the road fearfully cut up by waggon-wheels; so our wheels were nearly up to the axles in ruts. We got a capital luncheon at a small hotel and then went shopping.[80]

It was quite nice to wear a decent frock again and drive a good-looking pair of horses through a town. The worst of it was, our horses would not stand, so the people had to take a running shot at the buggy with their parcels. It amuses me the way we have to shake hands and say "How do you do" to all our shopkeepers, before any business can be done.[81] Our drive home was very enjoyable, and we got back about 7 o'clock.

We have been storing our potato crop, about 200 bushels off half an acre. Potatoes, and in fact everything which we don't want to have frozen, have to be stored in an underground cellar, at a depth of about eight feet. They dig a hole in the ground about eight feet deep, eight to ten feet long, and seven to eight feet wide. They then make a doorway with some steps going down into the hole and roof it all over, piling up the earth taken out to a height of four feet. The first houses in this country were made in the same way and [are] called "dug-outs."

October 10th. [1885]

Mrs. B— left us two or three days ago, to my great regret. It was so nice having someone to gossip to all the time I was working. She had rather a nasty accident on the way home. Her sister drove over from Three Forks to fetch her, lunched here, and, about 2:30, they started to go home.

It was bitterly cold. When they were about three miles from home, they came to a place where the road forked, both roads going to the same place, but one rather shorter than the other. They took the shortest road, though it was not the one by which Miss M— had come in the morning. This brought them to a creek; the usual crossing, where the water is wide and shallow, was frozen solid, and the ice like glass. The horses would not face it, so Mrs. B— tried to cross a little lower down at a narrow place, where the water was not frozen. The horses did not like this much better, at last one of them made a jump and the other held back. One never knows exactly how these things happen, but Miss M— was thrown out of the buggy, clean on to the bank; when she picked herself up, she saw Mrs. B— and the horses all struggling together in the water. She contrived to extract her sister; but, do what they would, they could not get the horses out.

Meanwhile Mrs. B—'s clothes were frozen as stiff as a board. So Miss M— pulled off her own dry shoes and stockings, and made Mrs. B— exchange her wet ones for these dry ones. She then took off her own wraps and piled them on to Mrs. B—, and started off to walk bare-footed, over gravel, sage brush, and prickly pear, to the nearest house for assistance. The owner, an American, refused to turn out; so there was nothing to be done, but to go back and bring Mrs. B— to the house, where the woman kindly supplied her with dry clothes.

Miss M— then walked home, and Mr. B— drove to the scene of the accident as hard as he could go. The horses and buggy were got out of the creek; curiously enough, no damage had been done. They all drove home, and, we hear, none of the party are any worse for the accident.

I've taken to cooking more now that the hot weather is gone, and invent all kinds of little puddings in a very simple way. They are considered wonderful productions, though, by the boys. That is one great thing in this country. Everything you cook is voted good, because everybody is well, and everybody is hungry. I potted a whole heap of eggs in dry salt in the summer, and have not found a bad one yet.

October 12th. [1885]

I am afraid you will think my last letter rather short, but I met with a nasty accident, which laid me up for some days, and I can only hobble about now. I was riding on the range with Jem, when the horse I was riding suddenly pitched on his head, and rolled on to my foot. When he got up, my foot was caught fast in the stirrup, but, by the greatest good luck, Frank had oiled the patent safety arrangement only the day before, so it acted all right, and my foot got free.[82] If I had had an ordinary stirrup, or the patent safety arrangement had not been in working order, I must have been killed, as my mount was a young "scarey" horse and would have dragged me for miles. As it was Jem had a hard job to catch him. When I got up, I found that I could not put my foot to the ground, and that it was giving me excruciating pain. What was to be done? Here we were, eight miles from the nearest house, and it seemed impossible to ride in such pain. However, as I refused to be left alone until Jem could go and fetch a conveyance, there was nothing for it but to mount as best I could, and ride to the nearest house. I would rather not have that ride over again!

The women at the ranche took me in hand, and were very kind. They thought there were no bones broken, and strongly advised Jem *not* to send for the doctor, as doctors, in their opinion, were not likely to do any good, but were quite certain to send in a long bill. Jem went home for the buggy, came back, and drove me home.

I was in great pain all night, so we telegraphed for the doctor, who came in the afternoon from Bozeman.[83] He seemed a very nice, clever man. He found that two toes were dislocated, but was not sure about the ankle; he put the toes in, which was a very painful operation, and then told me that I had better have ether while he examined the ankle, as he could then make a more thorough examination; so I had ether, and he found that the ankle was not actually dislocated, though very badly sprained. The doctor's fee of five guineas, which does not seem very outrageous for this country, as he had come eighteen miles, and could not get back that night.[84]

I am having a nice rest now, as the boys do everything and make most amusing nurses. Frank is cook and Jem is house-maid, &c. He *thinks* he is first-rate in the latter department, but I'm afraid there will be a great accumulation of dust when I get back to my duties again.

December 8th. [1885]

I think by the time you get this it will be Christmas. How quickly the year does seem to have gone! Next year I hope we may all be together in the old country.

Last year at this time we had deep snow and the thermometer down to 50 below zero. This year we have had
no snow at all down here, and the other day a chinook
cleared even the mountains. The weather is simply perfect,
the sun shining all day, and still quite warm. Everyone
says that the climate is getting less severe, and I suppose
the more the country gets settled the milder the winters
will become. At least, that seems to have been the case
in other Western States, so I don't see why Montana should
not follow suit.[85] All stock is looking fat and well; people
have not had to feed even their dairy stock. However,
some of our thorough-bred mares don't seem to agree
with this arrangement, for a whole lot of them came trooping
home from the range of their own accord the other day,
and now stand round the house and stables every morning,
looking sulky and evidently expecting to be fed.

We drove to Three Forks the other day in an hour and
twenty minutes. Jem calls it fourteen miles, so I think we
made good time.

All the English people down there were in ecstacies
over the result of the elections at home. Somehow or
other all the Englishmen out here seem to be staunch
Conservatives, which is a great loss to the party at home.[86]

Mr. H— and three others have just returned from a
month's hunt. They brought back about a ton of venison,
which they have been distributing amongst their friends.
We came in for a haunch of elk, which proved excellent,
such nice tender meat. One of the party shot an enormous
bull elk which fell down a precipice, so he had to content
himself with only getting the hide and the head. The
antlers are magnificent. Altogether the party were highly
delighted with their month's sport, as they got bear, elk,

and two or three kinds of deer, and had a very jolly time into the bargain, as there were five other Englishmen hunting in the district. They all camped together and, as you may imagine, had jolly nights round the camp-fire.

I have asked four Englishmen to come and dine and sleep on Christmas day, so we shall be a large party. They all bring their own blankets and sleep on the floor, as there is only one spare bed between them. They are to bring the turkey and we are going to kill a steer, which will provide the traditional sirloin and the suet for the pudding. It is rather an amusing way of giving a dinner for your guests to bring part of the provisions. As one winter is much the same as another out here, the description of our doings last winter will suffice for this.

February 20th. [1886]

The winter is nearly over now, we hope, so I am going to tell you a little about my experiences of a winter out here without servants. The worst part of it certainly is the getting up in the morning to light the fires; the house is so fearfully cold. One morning the thermometer in our drawing room registered ten below zero, which is as low as it goes. The bread was frozen solid and took an hour to thaw out before we could have breakfast. There is a stove in our bedroom, which Jem gets ready over night. First he cuts a lot of shavings, which are laid at the bottom of the stove, and on top of these a lot of dry wood; then the whole is sprinkled with parafin oil and ready to catch fire in a moment.[87]

About 7 o'clock in the morning Jem jumps up, lights the stove, and goes to bed again. In twenty minutes our room is as warm as possible; then we get up and dress.

Jem used to light the kitchen fire, which is also laid over-night, on his way to the stables, but as he was not very successful in getting it to burn, I do it myself now. While he is feeding the horses, I get breakfast ready and light the fire in the dining room. By the time breakfast is ready the rooms are warm. Stoves are certainly less trouble than fire-places, consume less wood, and warm a room very quickly. In the dining-room there is an "Angela" stove, which is very pretty, having a transparent front, so that you can see the fire or you can open the door in front, and then it is almost as good as an open fire-place. All this winter I have been out every day and feel tremen-dously well; in fact, I thoroughly enjoy the dry cold, though the boys rather grumble, at it.

Jem says, "It's all very fine, but it's no joke when the handles of the hay-forks burn your hands, unless you have gloves on, and you have to thaw a bit before you can put it in a horse's mouth, to prevent it from sticking to his tongue."

A young Englishman, during his first winter out here, doubted the latter fact, and experimented on his own tongue. The result was that when he felt the frozen steel burn, he snatched it away, and a small piece of his tongue came with it. The sceptic was converted. We either thaw the bits out in the oven, or dip them in water, before bridling a horse, which prevents them from sticking.

A horse's life out here during the winter in a stable can hardly be a happy one. The stables are desperately cold, being built of wood, often only a single half-inch plank. Ours are built of double boards, with a space of eight inches stuffed with straw between the boards; and yet, in the morning, in very cold weather, icicles hang from the horses' noses and eyelids, and their bodies are white with frost! In spite of this they do very well; even imported horses have wintered out here their first winter in sheds full of holes, and half the roof off, and have been none the worse for it.

It seems to me that horses don't mind *dry* cold in the least. I think if I was a Montana horse, I should prefer wintering out of doors to the stable. If they are out of doors they can move about to keep warm, and the very fact of having to paw for their food must help to keep up the circulation; but imagine being tied up and unable to move, in one of these desperately cold stables.

Jem had been amusing himself with bitting our two-year olds, saddling them up, and putting harness on them. He gets so interested that he forgets all about the cold, and will sit for an hour at a time, pipe in mouth, lost in admiration of some colt, which promises to carry himself in good form. Then, of course, I have to come out to help admire, and sometimes to put on or take off the tackle.

We generally tie up one front foot, when we begin breaking a colt, then he can't kick or strike, or get away from you; besides you can jump on his back, and he can't buck. You can do more with a colt in half an hour with his leg tied up, than you can in a week without it. As soon as they find they are in your power, they give up, and when they find you don't hurt them, they soon get gentle.

We have got any amount of little pigs running about—over fifty, and all white. They were born in the brush in the very coldest weather, forty below zero, and with five inches of snow on the ground. Most of them got their ears and tails frozen off, which gives them rather a grotesque appearance. The sows disappeared for a week, and never came near the house. What they lived on all that time I can't imagine. One old lady gobbled up a dead skunk, and made the whole place redolent for some days. I should have thought that no living animal would have eaten skunk; not even the man who said "he *could* eat turkey-buzzard, but didn't *hanker* after it."

It was a great joke getting these little pigs up to the house. About a week after a litter was born, the mother would come up to the house for something to eat. Then Jem would take a sack and follow her tracks, until he came to where the children were. I had to keep the old lady occupied by feeding her, while Jem caught the little ones and put them in the sack. He said it was very hard to catch them, as they would run out of the nest, and get buried in the snow, and run like mischief to put them in a warm sty, sometimes pursued by the old sow. These old sows are awfully fierce, and will attack a man in a minute.

February 25th. [1886]

Frank left us last week, to our very great regret, and now Jem has got a young Englishman, a very nice boy, to help him for a time. They are very busy breaking the yearlings to lead. I enjoy looking on, perched up on the top rail of the corral, and watching them lasso the little things, put halters on, and then go through a regular tug-of-war performance. They pull the colts about for a few minutes, just to show them what is wanted, and they tie them up all night, and let them teach themselves. In the morning the pupils have learnt their lesson, and will lead anywhere.

The weather is deliciously warm, and people all going about in their shirt-sleeves. Our young Englishman is a capital shot, and keen fisherman, so he keeps us well supplied with game and fish.

Jem went off the other day to look at some stock about a hundred miles from here, so I drove him down to Three Forks where he hired a buggy and team, and went on.[88] We started from here before the sun was up, and, as we drove along, the sunrise was most beautiful; much wonderful colours on the foot-hills and mountains. The main range of the Rockies was all covered with snow, sparkling and glistening in the sun; the lower range tinted with a lovely rose-colour, and the range below that a deep purple. Altogether the drive was very enjoyable. We arrived at Three Forks just as the B—s were finishing breakfast, so I stayed with them all day, and drove home in the evening.

One of the bridges which I had to cross had been damaged by the ice rising, when the latter broke up, as it always does in the spring.[89] They had been "fixing" this bridge all day, but hadn't finished it. One man had been left to look after it, and there he sat, calmly chewing tobacco, and whittling a stick—a Western man's sole amusement. I really think they are the best loafers under the sun. I called out to him to know what to do, upon which he said: "I guess you'll have to unhitch." So he helped me unhitch, and I led the horses, while he dragged the buggy across. We hitched up the horses again on the other side, holding an amicable conversation during the process, in the course of which he told me "he guessed I was pretty well used to horses," at which I felt flattered. I got home safely, and found the young Englishman ready to take the horses, and also that he had got dinner ready, being a very good cook. It seemed quite grand, as if one was at home with a full staff of servants.

Jem got home last night, having driven seventy miles that day, not bad travelling, and he said his horses were not over-tired either. These Western horses can do enormous distances in a day, and day after day without knocking up. Jem rode one fourteen-hand pony eighty-five miles between sunrise and sunset; and the same pony 450 miles in ten days, with fourteen stone on his back, and nothing to eat, except what grass he could get at the end of a picket rope.[90]

We are to have an old man, an American, to look after the horses (and to take care of me!) as Jem is going to Dakota soon with a batch of horses.

March 7th. [1886]

Here I am alone in my glory, with no one to look after me except old Van Vranken, the American, who is taking care of things while Jem is away.

A large bunch of horses arrived some days ago, and we have been very busy getting them ready for the Dakota market. Old Van is a capital hand at breaking horses, and we have been driving all day, sometimes Van and Jem, and sometimes I, go with one or other of them. About three inches of snow fell, so we were able to use bob sleighs. That is certainly a delightful way to get over the ground, though these young horses, with nothing to steady them, are apt to go rather faster than one intends; however, as they say out here, "we can ride as fast as they can run." And with the whole prairie to run over, it does not much matter where they go.

Jem nearly always gets me to drive, as he declares I have better hands for driving than he has, so I've had a most exciting time altogether. The day before the horses were shipped—which is a phrase here for sending things by train—two or three men came down to help, and the horses were all thrown, their tails plaited and sewn up in sacking to prevent them gnawing one another's tails or rubbing their own against the side of the truck. The poor things are only taken out of the truck and fed once in twenty-four hours, so you may imagine they are ready to eat horse-hair or anything else.

Some of them were such good-looking horses, that I was quite sorry to see them go. They stood from 15.2 to 16 hands, and I should not have been ashamed to drive some of them in England. The others were more of the omnibus stamp.[91]

I live by myself in one part of the house and Van by himself in another part. It is rather eerie at night. Being all alone, one notices all sorts of noises, that never bothered one before. The noise the rats make, the hooting of the owls, and the howling of the coyotes, even the squealing of the pigs, all make one feel rather jumpy. Of course I know I am in no danger, and old Van, though he is seventy-six years old, is a protection against tramps or anything of that sort, but still I don't quite like being alone. Old Van is a very amusing fellow, and looks on me as his grand-daughter, I think.

The other day I was going down to Three Forks, to call on a newly-married English-couple—or rather semi-English, for she's an American—and when I was quite ready, came out to the stables in a decent frock. Van seemed immensely struck with this, and stood gazing for a full minute; then, with a chuckle, said, "Well, we *are* fine." I daresay he was surprised at the transformation scene, as my ordinary get-up is all holes and patches. I am always burning holes in my skirts from going too near the stoves.

The people on whom I went to call seemed very nice, but she declares she can't live at Three Forks; so, after furnishing and fitting up a house there, he will have to leave and go to Helena. She was asking Mrs. B— all about housekeeping and how ladies manage out here. When Mrs. B— had finished, she said, "I hope I shall never come down to scrubbing *my* floors and cleaning *my* stoves." Mrs. B— piled it on after that.

Our pigs are increasing rapidly. There are about ninety now, all ages and sizes, running about. Van grumbles, as they make such a mess round the stables, and says "the ground is *paved* with pigs." And it certainly does look like it, when they are lying together in the sun. Thank goodness they don't bother me, as I always greet them with boiling water when they come round the kitchen door.

April 5th. [1886]

Jem came back a day or two ago. When he arrived I was staying at Three Forks, and as he did not come back until eleven o'clock at night, the house was all locked up, and he had to get in through the window. He was rather afraid that old Van would mistake him for a burglar or horse-thief, and pepper him with his shot gun, which he always keeps loaded with buck-shot in case of emergency.

I have had two men come down here fencing in about twenty acres of brush and rough pasture for the pigs. They fenced it with a stake and board fence, and we hope to keep the pigs in there until the autumn, and then turn them on to the peas to fatten. One of the men who is working at the fence, plays the violin very well; it is quite a treat to hear him. The men sleep in a tent and have their meals with old Van.

Little colts are coming pretty fast now. I ride slowly round the pastures every day, and take great interest in the new arrivals. It is so deliciously warm that my horse and I nearly go to sleep, and then I rouse him and myself up by jumping all the fences available.

We are all very much interested in the Home Rule question out here, but no argument is possible, as we are Conservative to a man. The Americans are all in favour of Home Rule; but it is no use arguing with them, as they don't really understand anything at all about it.[92] How I *should* like to be at home now and get all the news fresh. Of course we get all important news almost as soon as you do, but one misses all the items that lead up to a great event.

Jem talks of driving 300 head of horses back to the States, selling as he goes, until they are all sold. If he does, I shall come home, as I could not stay here for three or four months all alone. Some times I have a wild idea of going with him. It would be rather an adventure following the tails of 300 horses 1,500 miles, camping out every night, and shooting and fishing *en route.* They say that after the first fortnight the horses are no trouble at all, that the waggon carrying the tent, provisions, blankets, &c., goes first, and the horses all string out and follow it along the trail, with one or two men behind to keep them going. However, I'm afraid it would not really do for me to go, especially as I heard that some man in Texas, who took his wife and daughter with him on a long cattle-drive, had a difference with his "boys" on account of not letting them eat with his women-folk, whereupon they all left him; and there he was, 100 miles from anywhere, with 2,000 head of cattle and no one to handle them but himself, wife, and daughter. How he got out of the mess I never heard.

May 3rd. [1886]

Such a lovely day, quite hot and summery. I have just finished my house-work; it is now nearly 1 P.M., and I have been terribly busy since 6 o'clock this morning. Jem starts directly after breakfast every morning now, as he is riding on the horse round-up, and I don't see him again all day. I am going to ride with him to-morrow, which will be great fun. No sooner had he started this morning than Van comes to me, and, in a coaxing tone of voice, persuades me to jump on my horse and drive in a bunch of mares for him. I had such a nice ride round after them, and helped a man, whom I didn't know, to drive some cows, which he had found near our place, part of the way home. Then I drove our mares in, unsaddled my horse, and went and toiled at what Jem calls my "Fetish," *i.e.* house-cleaning.

I always clean out the drawing-room and bedroom on Mondays, filling up the hall with furniture, like the maids do at home. I think I do it in a very scientific way, and if I dust a single thing out of its turn, it quite puts me out. Just as I had got all the things nicely placed in the hall and could hardly open the front door, an Englishman living near us must needs come and call; so I invited him in, told him he would have to sit on the floor. He promised, instead, to come back when I had finished.

I must tell you what a splendid plan I have found for scrubbing the kitchen floor. No more going down on my hands and knees and scrubbing with a brush. Now I do it with a mop—made out of an old broom-handle and one of Jem's old flannel shirts—and a bucket of boiling water

with some lye in it. This I mop about the floor, and dry
it all up with a clean cloth. Lye is wonderful stuff, and
makes the boards as white as snow. I was so delighted
last Saturday when I found out what a success my new
plan was, as scrubbing that floor used to weigh on my
mind nearly all week.

We expect Harry Lowndes out this week from England,
and then I shall get my nice, cool, summer frocks. I find
holland in summer, and heavy thick serge in winter, are
the best stuff to wear out here.

Now the sun has gone down a bit, I am going to saddle
up and go on a private round-up on my own account. I
have just been up on the hill, and have seen hundreds of
horses being driven into the corral at the Horse Ranche;
so I expect Jem will be coming down here soon with a
bunch of ours, and will want me to help him. I am afraid I
shall only be able to ride this summer either very early or
very late, as even yesterday I found the sun rather too
much for my head, and I don't want to be affected by it
again, as I was last summer.

I forgot whether I told you all about the round-up
before. On a fixed day all the people who own horses on
the range meet at a certain place, and all ride off into the
hills. Then, when they have gone some miles, the captain
of the round-up tells them to spread out into a wide half-
circle and ride towards home, driving in all the horses
which they see. Presently the hills seem to be alive with
horses, all galloping in the same direction, with their manes
and tails flying in the wind, and the men all galloping after
them up and down hills and ravines, over badger-holes
and small dry water-courses. Now and then, though not
often, as the horses are so wonderfully clever over rough

ground, you see a man and horse turn a complete somer-
sault, the horse having put his fore-feet into a badger hole;
but this is only treated as a joke, and the fallen generally
pick themselves up none the worse, and are at it again.
Sometimes a band of horses strike back for the hills,
which treats you to a glorious gallop to head them off.
Altogether it is most exciting. As they get near the corral
the separate bunches become merged into one huge band,
and you can see nothing but hundreds of horses galloping,
and clouds of dust. Then two or three men on the fastest
horses gallop on ahead, let down the bars of the corral,
and stand in front of the horses to turn them in. On they
come, until they are headed by these men. When they begin
huddling together, circling round, getting their heads turned
the wrong way, and acting generally in the most provoking
manner possible. "Bronchos" seem to have the greatest
objection to going into a corral.

Very often an old gentle horse, who no more minds
going into the corral than into his own stable, stands just
in the gateway, blocking it up, and looking as if he was
frightened to death at going in; till you long to be near
him with a good thick stick. At last a few make up their
minds to go in. The rest follow pell-mell like a flock of
sheep; the bars are put up, saddle horses led away reeking
with sweat, and tied up to a post, with a forty-pound sack
on their backs to rest (?); and cutting out, which I have
told you about before, begins.

When this is all over, the "boys" indulge in a little fun.
Some one or other has got a four-year-old "broncho" which
he wants ridden; accordingly some enterprising individual
offers to ride him, if the "boys" will make up a purse to
see the fun. So the hat goes round, and is soon returned

with a contribution of eight or nine dollars; not bad pay for riding a "broncho" once. Half a dozen lassoes are soon whirling in the air; the luckless "broncho" is caught by the forelegs, and comes down with a thud that might be heard a hundred yards away; someone jumps on his head, a bit is forced into his mouth, and, for the first time in his life, he finds himself bridled. A handkerchief is then fastened over his eyes to blindfold him, and he receives a hearty kick in the ribs, or someone jumps with both feet on his side, as a friendly (?) intimation to get up [*sic*]. As soon as he is on his legs, a heavy Mexican saddle is clapped onto his back, and the girths drawn as tight as possible.[93] Then he is hauled outside the corral with a running accompaniment of kicks and blows. The "broncho" rider climbs gingerly into the saddle, leans forward to pull off the handkerchief, then settles himself well back in the saddle, and, if the broncho does not start at once, plunges the heavy Mexican spurs into the unfortunate animal's shoulders, and away they go; the quadruped bucking and bawling, or running for dear life, and the biped whooping, yelling, flogging, and spurring to his heart's content. A rough school, and no wonder that the young idea [*sic*] takes to buck-jumping as naturally as a duck to water.

July 10th. [1886]

I think by this time my letters will have given you a fair idea of a lady's life in the Far West, with its daily routine.[94]

Now I am going to give you a resume of this summer, and then I shall have brought a history of nearly two years to a close. To begin with, I have been alone nearly the whole summer. After the horse round-up, Jem was away all the time shipping horses, except for one or two days, at intervals of three or four weeks; so there I was with old Van, the horses, and the pigs. But you must not imagine that the time hung heavily on my hands. On the contrary, I was busy from morning to night. Lonely I was, of course, as sometimes I did not see a soul except Van, who was always very good, for days at time. When I say Van was good, I mean he was nice to me; otherwise I had to do what he ought to have done, for he was old and very loth to get on a horse, so I did all the riding.

Every morning at ten o'clock I used to turn the whole band of horses, which we keep on our own ranche, outside the gates to graze; then at one o'clock I rode about three or four miles to see that they were not straying off back to the hills; then again at night I rounded them all up and brought them home. The pigs also were no small source of annoyance, for they were always getting out, and into mischief. So I had to spend half my time chasing them home again. I used to carry them several buckets full of potatoes every day, and feed them inside the fence, by way of keeping them contented. You would have laughed to see me, leaning over the pig-fence, with a bucketful of potatoes in my hand, uttering unearthly yells of "Piggy, pig, piggy!" to call them to the feast. Besides this, I used to ride round the fences every night to see that they were all right; so you may imagine that, with all this and the house, I had enough to do.

The evenings were the worst part of it. It was so fear-fully lonely, sitting all by oneself. Of course I had my piano, and Jem sent me books every week, and there were the English papers, but still these are not company; even my dog "Rook" and black cat "Jack" seemed more satisfactory in that respect. About once a week some of the Englishmen would come to call, and I made the acquaintance of a "granger's" wife, whom I visited nearly every day to get milk (as our cow is dry); but, of course, this did not lessen the loneliness of my evenings. I don't think I could stand another summer alone, it is so trying to one's nerves.

I had eventually to sell all the pigs, as it was impossible to keep them in; so I rode about trying to find customers for them, and a hard job it was, for, of course, no one wants to buy pigs in the middle of summer. However, I triumphed at last, and got rid of them all at some price or another. It was a great satisfaction when I saw the last batch go off in the waggon. I managed better with my horses, as I was able to keep them together, and I must say I love that work; it is so interesting to watch the little colts growing, and I know every animal in the herd. In the evenings I often used to take a panful of salt, and get the whole band round me; even the shyest in the whole band eventually came up to me to get its share.

Our big black horse was taken very ill with pneumonia, and I was dreadfully anxious about him. He was so weak one day that I thought he must die; so I told Van that the horse wanted stimulants, and nothing else would save him. Van said he didn't know what to do, he daren't leave the horse, and there were no stimulants in the house; so I saddled up Sinister, my cowpony, and galloped up to town, went straight to the saloon, and asked for a bottle of whiskey. I don't know what the bar-keeper thought. The horse began to mend as soon as he had the whisky, and eventually got well. But when our bill came in from the "store," we found a bottle of whiskey charged against us every day for a month! We never knew how much of it the horse got! If he got it at all, I am surprised that he is alive; for they say this Western whisky is fearful stuff, in fact, the natives call it, "Kill at forty rods!"

Jem came home on my birthday, and said that I must go back to England at once, for he should have to be away on and off until November, and I must not be left alone here any longer; so I am really coming home. Jem is going to move all our best horses to a new range, about eleven miles from here, and put a man in charge. We have let this ranche to two Englishmen, and arranged everything, so that I can go home at once, and Jem will follow in December.[95]

Of course, I am fearfully busy, packing up all my household goods, and getting ready to start, and awfully excited about coming home. I shall be sorry to leave this country, and the ranche, and all my pets; but, of course, it will be delicious to see everybody at home again, and I am very curious to see how I shall like the old life after a long absence from it.

February 20th. [1887]

Here I am back in England again. The journey was most enjoyable, and everyone was very kind to me. We had a capital passage, and landed at Glasgow all right. The old country was looking so beautiful, the bright green of the fields and trees so refreshing after the brown, dried-up appearance of the prairie. The scenery of the Rockies is very grand certainly, and the vastness of America very impressive; but for quiet beauty, and a delicious sense of rest, comfort, and home life, it cannot compare with England.

I have been home some months now, and enjoy it all very much; but, all the same, I long for my active, busy life out West. I have never been so well, and could not have been happier anywhere, than I was during my two years out there, and the best proof of this is that I am longing to be back again, and look forward to the day when I shall set foot on the great ocean steamship, and set my face once more towards my mountain home in the Rockies.

I.R.

Epilogue
"My Active, Busy Life"

A s she explains in the last real letter of what became her book, while James was off selling the stock through the autumn of 1886, Isabel returned home to Britain. Assuming she made no long stops or detours on her return, the itinerary would probably have been a reverse of their trip west made two years earlier: from Moreland on the Northern Pacific Rail Road to St. Paul and Chicago, thence again by rail to New York, by oceangoing steamship to Glasgow, and by rail again and finally coach to the family home. Assuming also that she left soon after her last letter was posted, this estimate would put her home at Holdenhurst in the final weeks of August 1886. James joined her in Britain before the end of the year.

For several months after her return Isabel certainly relaxed and idled away her time, undoubtedly regaling the family and friends with the full stories of what she mentions in the letters and perhaps even demonstrating her newly won skills at housekeeping and cooking—or maybe not,

since at the FitzHerberts' there would have been proper
domestic servants on hand again. Isabel's adventure would
certainly have sensitized her to the accounts of others who
had made similar stays in the American West. Though
she may have been aware of one particular book before
she left in 1884, it is possible that she either encountered
Isabella Bird's well-known work *A Lady's Life in the Rocky
Mountains,* which had just come out in a new edition while
she was in New York, or that she became acquainted with
one of the earlier London editions once she returned home.[1]
Sometime during that autumn of 1886 came the kernel of
an idea to collect her own letters into a similar work. A
decision to pursue publication can be fixed to a date no
later than the final entry given in her book, February 20,
1887. This "letter" is more of an epilogue, obviously written
in England specifically to conclude the book. How Isabel
went about editing her letters and whether she approached
W. H. Allen & Company before or after her manuscript
was complete, are unanswerable questions. Allen & Company was an obvious venue, however. The London publisher
already had a series of works by and about women in print
and inserted a double-page ad for "Health Primers" and
the "Eminent Women" series in the back of Isabel's book.

Considering carefully the book's characteristics, it is
tempting to conclude that Isabel may never have intended
copies to be available in Montana. First, though she was
obviously pleased with her work, she used only her initials
as a byline on the title page, choosing not to publish it
over her own name. If nothing else, this insured that there
would be no immediate fallout if it were ill received. Second,
whereas Isabella Bird left names in place in her work, Isabel
Randall purged personal names, albeit somewhat carelessly.

Finally, it is evident from what remains that her editing cut out a great deal of the letters' original text. Since these were private letters, Isabel may have realized that some of her original comments were less than flattering to their subjects. She may have been looking for a measure of plausible deniability. Elizabeth Hampsten points out that at the time even women's private writings tended to emphasize the much-valued qualities of "progress," a conclusion that can be applied to Isabel's letters.[2] Certainly as the compiler of her private correspondence she would wish to polish and present her experiences in the most positive light. Isabel also struck the year from each letter. This last little conceit was a popular device that kept a printed work from becoming outdated too quickly.

As she notes in the book's conclusion, Isabel intended to stay at home in England only briefly. She was eager to return to her "active, busy life" on her Montana horse ranch. We do not know exactly when she and James returned to Montana, but it would likely have been in the late spring or early summer of 1887. Upon arriving they would have found the prospects of the Moreland Ranch Stock Company much changed from those when she left. By making their trip home to Britain they had chanced to avoid the disastrous winter of 1886–87, the season that bankrupted so many livestock firms in the West and spelled an effectual end to the open-range stock industry. It affected the Randall's fortunes as well. As a result, James's position with the Moreland Ranch Stock Company was evolving. At about the same time that Isabel's book was in press, James deeded more than a thousand acres under his trusteeship directly to the firm itself. Nine months later he made a trip to Helena, where over several days most of the rest of the property he held as trustee—nearly three thousand acres more, along with water rights and his interest in the Moreland Canal—was transferred to the company as well.[3] Beyond these transactions we have no record of the fortunes or misfortunes of the Moreland Ranch Stock Company until the firm disbanded. Of the Randall's second stay in the Gallatin Valley we know little more, all of it directly relating to the local reception of Isabel's book.

Once *A Lady's Ranche Life in Montana* was in print in Britain, copies of Isabel's book inevitably made their way to the Gallatin Valley. Though it was published in 1887, no book notices or reviews appeared in Britain or the United States. There was no local comment on the book by "I. R." at all until 1889. Precisely how many books got to Montana and how they arrived is not known, but it is probable that it took time, perhaps more than a year. Given their later responses, it is possible that local residents had not seen the book until that late date. Unfortunately this is all conjecture. The only facts available are that one book, and probably more, arrived in or before 1889. But someone stumbled across Isabel's book and brought or sent copies to the Gallatin Valley, where it seems to have circulated quickly from hand to hand.

For a time the author's identity remained unknown, but given the opinions of her neighbors printed in the work, reactions were predictable. Many in Moreland and the county's other small communities were indignant. Finally in mid-March of 1889 a telltale notice, couched in the journalistic style common at the time, appeared in one of Bozeman's two local newspapers, the *Avant Courier.* "Mrs. J. Randall, who lives on the old Culver ranch, near

Moreland," it read, "and who is the author of a work on ranch life in the Gallatin Valley, advertises her personal property for sale and will make a trip to New Zealand."[4] It was one sentence, a combination advertisement and society report. But the literary measures Isabel had employed to guard her anonymity proved insufficient to cover her tracks. The claim of a trip to New Zealand was perhaps outlandish enough to have been a ruse. There were other Englishwomen in the valley, but this terse note pointed a finger at the offending author of the book people were talking about. After this, life became positively difficult for James and Isabel.

In addition to James's declining fortunes as a stock rancher, the couple now had to weather the blast of chilly ostracism from what small society Moreland offered. Isabel's comments bit deeply into the community's pride and economic optimism. Within a month someone determined to bite back. It came in the form of a stinging doggerel, published barely four weeks after the first notice publicly identified the author of *A Lady's Ranche Life.* The "Rustic Artiste's" derisive "Composite Photo of the Lady" stood as a comment on Isabel's social errors by cataloging the half-successes and failures of daily routine she chose not to mention in her published letters.

A Composite Photo of the Lady
Whose Ranch Life
Has Lately Been "Chronicled."

Is she dainty and sweet, the lady I. R.?
Whose life-tale is wafted both near and afar;
Is her foot-fall as light as the thistles' snow,

When it sprinkles the sunlit sward? Ah! no!
A lumbering gait, and muscles like "Sullivan,"
And her strength is shown as she wields the rein,
Both as charioteer and equestrienne,
E'en Jem suffers reining, some venture to say,
In a homeopathic, henpecked way;
But, in wedlock, t'is ever a matter of chance
Which one of the parties will carry the pants.

Perhaps, she has matchless beauty of face,
Encompassed by tresses of curving grace;
But to paragons are given the leases
To pick all the rest of the world to pieces,
Alas for the fame of "Medusa" of old!
If "Perseus" now lived a new tale would be told;
'Tis well she evinces enough of pride,
When approached by her sex, to run and hide.[5]
Ye "natives," possessed of such mystical art!
Can you not to this sister a secret impart?
That through "powder" or "warpaint" some clue
    can be got,
Under which of the races this alien to jot.
We cannot say black, that she never has been
Nor can the Caucasians lay claim to her kin,
Unless she would follow one simple behest
And scour her rust in the flour chest.[6]

A servant she had, in her papers we read,
In the breasts of the neighbors strong envy to breed;
And they schemed and planned, in their jealous rage,
But, lo, we are turning another page,
On a "native's" threshold, with outstretched hands,

A fainting, famishing cripple stands,
And soon, too soon has the tale untwisted
That a "Sally Brass" in our midst existed.[7]
Kitchen-maid, parlor-maid, tender of swine,
Form a combination hard to define;
And when laundress and butter-maid, too, we annex,
The picture must certainly be most complex;
But, with foresight so keen and pencil so deft
She has furnished the scenes we, in fine, would
    have left.
Such candor as hers may be well to possess;
For she openly boasts of what few would confess,
Where reverence, pity and sympathy, want,
'T were no flattering thing for a woman to vaunt.

She is butter-maid, now, so the woman may call
With impunity, since they both hold the same stall,
And off to the grocer in queer little cakes
Is carried the substance for butter she makes.
A chunk to the tavern has found its way,
To act as a riddle day after day;
Where all are invited to venture a guess,
'Till the treat has 'round, at the gray-white mess;
But no one as yet, whether calm, or a flutter,
Was stupid enough to pronounce it butter.
Lady, do not despair though you fail to attain
Perfection, at first, you may yet try again;
'T were a safer end, for a wit like thee,
Than to hope for a seat, 'mongst the literati.

We have seen her at church and the proof is given
That her thoughts labored nearer to earth than heaven

Once her posture, while trying a snort to suppress,
Occasioned an unlucky split in her dress,
And the linen that peeped through this crevice of fate,
Had long lost a claim to immaculate.
Her shuffling and punching of Jem in the rib,
With the phases exposed on her prominent jib,
And the tatters that swung from her petticoat braid
All went in the side-show my lady displayed,
O had the gift not been then withheld her!
She would scarce have inflicted her satire weak
On those once regaled with a farce so unique.

Now we see her at last as she enters the train,
On the back of her ulster, a large grease stain,
We will leave it the rest of the story to tell,
While the "natives" extend her a long farewell.

RUSTIC ARTISTE.[8]

Newspapers were the primary means of broadcasting at this time. The poem's appearance there would have insured that virtually everyone in the Gallatin Valley got a laugh at "the Lady's" expense. Nearly twenty years earlier another English traveler, Barham Zincke, noted that Americans did not chafe at acknowledging superior "intellect or refinement—provided the possessor was not 'putting on airs.'" Assuming superiority, however, was "a sin against equality, which is never forgiven in this world, and which every American trusts will not be forgotten in the next."[9] For their part, Gallatin Valley residents misunderstood the stratigraphic realities of Isabel's cultural background as badly as she misinterpreted the social democracy of the late American frontier. While Isabel was merely reporting her interpretations of what were, to her, the curious social conventions of a foreign culture, she probably did not harbor negative opinions about her neighbors. If guilty of anything, Isabel Randall was guilty of being tactless in print.

The appearance of the poem in the local news sheet was probably a proverbial last straw for the Randalls. With their fortunes and those of the Moreland Ranch Stock Company ebbing ever lower, and now all but exiles on their 160 acres, the couple determined to return to England, this time together. In preparation, James again mortgaged their ranch to his uncle to finance the return.[10]

The people of Moreland were unwilling to let the effendi simply pick up and slip away that easily. In June, Isabel's skulking visit to Moreland was noted as a sarcastic society notice in the paper. "Mrs. James Randall was in the burgh Monday, but for some unknown reason failed to call on her numerous (?) lady friends," it read. Then it drove the point home: "Mrs. Randall is the author of 'My Lady's Ranch Life.'"[11] A comment elsewhere in the same issue provides the clearest contemporary statement of the perspective of the Randalls' Montana neighbors.

> Mrs. Perks of Moreland says the subject matter of "The Lady's Ranch Life" created no little excitement and comment in the neighborhood, and made the author thereof an unenviable reputation. The ladies of Gallatin Valley have a right to feel indignant, as the writer's ridicule and unwarranted statements had no foundation in fact and were intended to cast slurs on the integrity and virtue of a class of ladies far superior in intellect, culture, and refinement to her English

"ladyship" (?) [sic]. Little did she know when making these accusations about the "natives" that they would be hurled back again at the author with greater force than they were received. The ladies of Montana are too brave and noble to sit down and quietly submit to accusations against their good name without resenting them and we glory in their grit. "Tenderfeet" will take notice and govern themselves accordingly.[12]

This minor paragraph in the newspaper seems to have reflected general sentiments in Moreland and Bozeman. It was a humiliating rebuke to the general liberties Isabel had taken when displaying snobbery at their expense before the world.

James and Isabel determined to stick it out long enough to conclude the season's meager harvest, perhaps to demonstrate that they would not be run out of town but also because the harvest afforded them the opportunity to settle any outstanding accounts. Probably one of James's last acts as a stockholder in the Moreland Ranch Stock Company was to register formally the riparian claims for the water needed to irrigate MRSC property.[13]

Late in 1889 James and Isabel Randall left their ranch to drive the mile into Moreland one final time. Beside the track they stood on the platform of the same tiny railroad station at which they had arrived so optimistically in 1884. The east-bound Northern Pacific train pulled in from Logan and Three Forks, and the couple boarded the coach while their trunks and boxes were heaved into the baggage car. Brakes were released, the whistle shrieked twice, and with a chuffing lurch the train steamed toward the next stop a few miles east at Central Park. It is tempting to wonder if, as the train crossed the bridge over the Gallatin River bottom, Isabel looked downstream toward the house she was leaving. They had not managed to sell their own quarter-section ranch before leaving.[14] Perhaps they could not find a buyer; it is possible that they were merely planning an extended but temporary trip home, hoping that given time, the animosity over *A Lady's Ranche Life in Montana* would blow over. It probably did, but Isabel FitzHerbert Randall never returned to find out for sure.

Notes

Foreword

1. James S. Brisbin, *The Beef Bonanza; or, How to Get Rich on the Plains, Being a Description of Cattle-Grazing, Sheep Farming, Horse-Raising and Dairying in the West* (Philadelphia: Lippincott, 1881), 24–25, 133–37.

2. The text to this song can be located at http://www.traditionalmusic.co.uk/nwc_tunebook/songs/Starving_To_Death_On_My_Government_Claim.txt (accessed June 18, 2003).

3. The question of whether women suffered more than men in the West has been fiercely debated in the past. Obviously women at varying times in different parts of the West had dissimilar experiences. Deborah Fink's *Agrarian Women: Wives and Mothers in Rural Nebraska, 1880–1940* (Chapel Hill: University of North Carolina Press, 1992) finds evidence of hardship, loneliness, and disappointments. Other historians, such as Sandra Myers, in *Westering Women and the Frontier Experience: 1800–1915* (Albuquerque: University of New Mexico Press, 1982), see the female experience in a more positive light and argue that women embraced the possibility of advancement in the West despite their return to

a more primitive lifestyle at least in the beginning. Linda Williams Reese views the frontier experience of women as one that made them partners on the land, but she also notes the sacrifices they were obliged to make. See *Women of Oklahoma, 1890–1920* (Norman: University of Oklahoma Press, 1997). For an excellent overview of women's experiences on farms and ranches, see Glenda Riley, *The Female Frontier: A Comparative View of Women on the Prairie and the Plains* (Lawrence: The University Press of Kansas, 1987).

4. Nancy Woloch, *Women and the American Experience,* 3rd ed. (Boston: McGraw-Hill Higher Education, 2000), 275–306, provides perhaps the best succinct summary of the "new woman" in America. For information on the English "new woman," see Joan Perkin, *Victorian Women* (New York: New York University Press, 1993), 241. Elizabeth Seymour Eschbach compares and contrasts higher education for women in England and the United States in *The Higher Education of Women in England and America, 1865–1920,* Women's History and Culture, vol. 6 (New York: Garland Publishing, 1993).

5. Joan Perkin, *Women and Marriage in Nineteenth-Century England* (Chicago: Lyceum Books, 1989), 246–47. See also Perkin, *Victorian Women,* 235–48.

6. This was a strategy both the Democrats and the Republicans used in the 1880s and 1890s in foreign affairs regarding British interests in Latin America and elsewhere. See Joseph A. Fry, "Phases of Empire: Late Nineteenth-Century U.S. Foreign Relations," in *The Gilded Age: Essays on the Origins of Modern America,* ed. Charles W. Calhoun (Wilmington, Del.: Scholarly Resources, 1996), 273–75.

7. Catharine Beecher stated in her best-selling and often reprinted domestic advice book that Americans considered being a servant worse than slavery. See *A Treatise on Domestic Economy for the Use of Young Ladies at Home and at School* (Boston: Marsh, Capen, Lyon, and Webb, 1941), 200.

8. Nell Irvin Painter gives good information on America's class structure. See *Standing at Armageddon: The United States,*

1877–1919 (New York: W. W. Norton, 1987), xvii–xlvi; for information on social mobility in America, see Howard P. Chudacoff and Judith E. Smith, *The Evolution of American Urban Society,* 3rd ed. (Englewood Cliffs, N.J.: Prentice Hall, 1988), 142–44.

9. An insightful work on the development of nineteenth-century ethnology is Robert Bieder, *Science Encounters the Indian, 1820–1880: The Early Years of American Ethnology* (Norman: University of Oklahoma Press, 1986).

10. Elizabeth Bacon Custer, *"Boots and Saddles"; or, Life in Dakota with General Custer* (1885; reprint, Norman: University of Oklahoma Press, 1961), 60.

Introduction

1. Robert G. Athern, *Westward the Briton* (Lincoln: University of Nebraska Press, 1971), 185–202; Daniel J. Boorstin, "Introduction," in Isabella L. Bird, *A Lady's Life in the Rocky Mountains,* ed. Daniel J. Boorstin (Norman: University of Oklahoma Press, 1960), xx–xxi.

2. Randall was not the only female writer to ride Bird's coattails. The year after her book became available, *A Lady's Experience in the Wild West in 1883* (London: G. Tucker, 1888) by Lady Rose Pender (who really was of the English nobility) appeared before the public. Similar titles by other authors followed. Moira O'Neill wrote an account of her residence on a Canadian outfit titled "A Lady's Life on a Ranche," which appeared in the January 1898 issue of *Blackwood's Edinburgh Magazine.*

3. Samuel Taylor Coleridge, *Table-Talk,* August 14, 1831, quoted in *A New Dictionary of Quotations on Historical Principles,* ed. H. L. Mencken (New York: Alfred A. Knopf, 1962).

4. Dee Garceau, *The Important Things of Life: Women, Work, and Family in Sweetwater County, Wyoming, 1880–1929* (Lincoln: Nebraska University Press, 1997), 89–111.

5. Frederick Jackson Turner, "The Significance of the Frontier in American History," in *The Frontier in American History* (Tucson: University of Arizona Press, 1986); Patricia Limerick,

The Legacy of Conquest: The Unbroken Past of the American West (New York: W. W. Norton, 1987); cf. Richard W. Etulain, *Re-Imagining the Modern American West: A Century of Fiction, History, and Art* (Tucson: University of Arizona Press, 1996), which provides a good overall discussion of the differences between these interpretations and the historiography of each.

6. Elizabeth Hampsten, *Read This Only to Yourself: The Private Writings of Midwestern Women, 1880–1910* (Bloomington: Indiana University Press, 1982), 88–89, 94–95.

7. Emily French, *Emily: The Diary of A Hard-Worked Woman,* ed. Janet Lecompte (Lincoln: University of Nebraska Press, 1987); Nannie Alderson, *A Bride Goes West* (Lincoln: University of Nebraska Press, 1969); Mrs. Nat Collins, *The Cattle Queen of Montana,* ed. Alvin E. Dyer (Spokane, Wash.: Dyer Printing Co., [1900?])

8. Athern, *Westward the Briton,* xi.

9. "Tizinctvn" appeared by name as early as William's taxation census, recorded in the Domesday Book (fol.274a col.1), in John Pym Yeatman, *Feudal History of the County of Derby,* vol. 1 (London: Bumrose & Sons, [1886]), 37. The estate was acquired as a dower when one of the Fitzherberts married into the even more ancient Abini (Abney) family.

10. George Edward Cockayne, *Complete Baronetage,* vol. 5, 1707–1800 (Exeter, England: William Pollard & Co., 1906), 245; Barbara M. Smith, *A History of the Fitzherbert Family* (London: Minerva Press, 1995); Thomas Williams, *A Short History of Tissington and Its Parish Church,* rev. D. H. Buckley (Ashbourne, England: D. H. Buckley, 1965). The rank of baronet is the most junior hereditary entitlement, created by James I in 1611 and bestowed most generally upon the heads of landed families. A baronet is addressed by the honorific title "Sir," and the title descends indefinitely by male primogeniture, but neither a baronet nor the family is considered ennobled. The family does not enter the peerage, he is not addressed as "Lord" nor his wife as "Lady," nor may he fill a seat in Parliament's upper body, the House of Lords, unless the regent elevates a baronet to a higher station as (in ascending order) baron, viscount, earl, marquis, or duke. Only

princes of the royal house rank above a duke. Below a baronet rank knights, whose titles do not descend, and the rest of those claiming quality (or at least wealth) without rank—the untitled aristocracy, known sniffily as "gentlemen." Even had her father inherited the FitzHerbert title, Isabel would never have been properly known as "Lady Randall" except by her American neighbors, and then using the term only as an epithet. Isabel's husband's family held no position other than that of clerical respect.

11. J. A. Venn, *Alumni Cantabrigienses,* part 2, vol. 2 (Cambridge, England: Cambridge University Press, 1944), 511; Arthur Charles Fox-Davis, *Armorial Families: A Directory of Gentlemen of Coat-Armour,* vol. 1 (1929; reprint, Charles E. Tuttle, 1970), xxviii; obituary, *The Times* (London), August 1, 1894.

12. Mrs. Randall did not spell her given name I-S-A-B-E-L-L-E, as appears in most American comments on her work. A cataloger in the British Museum (now the British Library) is probably the original source of the misspelling. The error has been perpetuated in print at least since the publication of Robert Athern's bibliography in *Westward the Briton* (Lincoln: University of Nebraska Press, 1953), and the first edition of Wright Howes's *U.S.iana* (New York: R. R. Bowker for Newberry Library, 1954), which listed her book (R-49) but also misspelled her name.

13. "The Greaves Family of Beeley, Derbyshire, England," Gen.288, Graves Family Association, Wrentham, Mass.; 1881 Census (Britain) for Holdenhurst, Hampshire County, microform edition (Salt Lake City: Church of Jesus Christ of Latter-day Saints, 1982), 5952.

14. David M. Waller, "Justices of the Peace," *The Oxford Companion to Law* (Oxford, England: Clarendon Press, 1980); 1881 Census (Britain), Hampshire County, microform ed., 5952.

15. In 1868 Richard William Randall left Sussex for a living at All Saint's Church in Clifton, Gloucestershire. Afterward elevated to canon at Berks Cathedral (a position once held by his father), he finally ascended to the deanship of Chichester, from which he retired in 1892. Randall composed several devotional

and meditative works as well as a notable commentary, *Life in the Catholic Church,* which passed through several editions. Obituary, *The Times* (London), December 24, 1906. James Leslie Randall, Richard's younger brother, progressed through churchly appointments to conclude his own career as Bishop of Reading. *Crockford's Clerical Directory* (1890), 1061. One brother between them, William Lowndes Randall (1832–), pursued a military career and may have been the contact that allowed Isabel's son, Basil, to pursue one as well. Addiscombe Cadet Papers, British Library.

16. Cyril Wilberforce Randall (b. 1856) matriculated to Magdalen College the same year James graduated, and Francis Henry Randall (b. 1858)—who eventually followed James westward to Montana—matriculated to Keble the following year. Neither remained at school to take his degree. Joseph Foster, *Alumni Oxonienses, the Members of the University of Oxford, 1715–1886,* vol. 3 (London: Parker & Co., 1888), 1173–74.

17. 1881 Census (Britain) for Clifton, Gloucestershire, 1908.

18. Those interested in the English in Montana will wish to compare Isabel Randall's account with Donna M. Lucey, *Photographing Montana, 1894–1928: The Life and Work of Evelyn Cameron* (New York: Knopf, 1990).

19. Alderson, *Bozeman,* 15; McElrath, *Yellowstone Valley,* 57, quote cited in Ernest Staples Osgood, *The Day of the Cattle Man* (Chicago: University of Chicago Press, 1960), 83. Primary and secondary source material on the stock boom is voluminous, but scant attention has been paid to stock raising in recent scholarship. Osgood's is still considered the best overall work. Good surveys and basic bibliographies of the livestock industry appear in Malone, Roeder, and Lang's *Montana: A History of Two Centuries,* rev. ed. (Seattle: University of Washington Press, 1976), 145–71, and in James M. Hamilton's *History of Montana: From Wilderness to Statehood,* 2nd ed., ed. Merrill G. Burlingame (Portland, Ore.: Binsfords & Mort, 1970), 384–412. Good primary-source bibliographies can be found in the Osgood book; Edward Everett Dale, *The Range Cattle Industry: Ranching on the Great Plains from 1865 to 1925,* new ed. (Norman: University of Oklahoma Press,

1960); and Michael P. Malone et al., *Montana: A History of Two Centuries,* rev. ed. (Seattle: University of Washington Press, 1991).

20. Thomson P. McElrath, *The Yellowstone Valley: What it is, Where it is, and How to Get to It. A Hand-book for Tourists and Settlers* (St. Paul, Minn.: St. Paul Book and Stationery Company, 1880), 56.

21. Matt W. Alderson, *Bozeman: A Guide to Its Places of Recreation and a Synopsis of Its Superior Natural Advantages, Industries, and Opportunities* (Bozeman, Mont.: Avant Courier [?], 1883). Alderson specifically contrasted Montana's laissez-faire ranching and farming opportunities with the burdensome English agricultural realities of rents, taxes, and tithes.

22. James S. Brisbin, *The Beef Bonanza; or, How to Get Rich on the Plains* (1881; reprint, Norman: University of Oklahoma Press, 1959), 158–65; William Baillie-Grohman, "Cattle Ranches of the Far West," *The Fortnightly Review* 34 (October 1, 1880): 438–57. There were scores of others, however.

23. This belief was general but was stated explicitly by F. Barham Zincke in *Last Winter in the United States: Being Table Talk Collected During a Tour Through the Late Southern Confederation, the Far West, the Rocky Mountains* (1868; reprint, Freeport, N.Y.: Books for Libraries Press, 1970), 237–38.

24. Brisbin, *Beef Bonanza,* 159. He does not state his sources.

25. An excellent summary of the investment side of the boom is provided in Gene M. Gressley, *Bankers and Cattlemen* (New York: Alfred A. Knopf, 1966).

26. *Gallatin Valley Gazetteer* (1892), 39. County population nearly doubled, from 3,643 to 6,246.

27. *Weekly Chronicle (Bozeman, Mont.),* March 15, 1883. The steep, temporary tracks over the pass were removed upon completion of the Bozeman Tunnel, which cut under the summit, officially completed January 22, 1884. Peter Koch, "Historical Sketch: Bozeman, Gallatin Valley, and Bozeman Pass," in *Gallatin Valley Gazetteer and Bozeman City Directory, 1892–93, including Belgrade,* vol. 1 (Bozeman: J. D. Radford, 1892).

28. *Avant Courier (Bozeman, Mont.)*, April 5, 1883.

29. James Randall's arrival would undoubtedly appear in the New York port records, but during this age of emigration they are so voluminous that an effective search cannot be made. Randall could have disembarked at New York as early as mid-1881 and as late as March 1883.

30. *Weekly Chronicle (Bozeman, Mont.)*, June 13, 1883. Hamilton dates from 1868, when a post office was established there. A. C. Peale of the first Hayden survey passed through town in 1871 and noted that it had a "dozen houses." It had probably not grown much in thirteen years. Today the small Meadow View Cemetery is the original town's only remnant. *Yellowstone and the Great West: Journals and Letters of the 1871 Hayden Expedition,* ed. Marlene Deahl Merrill (Lincoln: University of Nebraska Press, 1999), 183–84.

31. Dennis Swibold, "Manhattan Plans Big 100th Birthday Party," *Bozeman Chronicle,* September 21, 1984.

32. Deed dated October 22, 1883, Mortgage deeds, vol. 7, 154–55, Gallatin County Clerk and Recorder's Office, Bozeman, Mont. Volume and page numbers are hereafter given in the form "7:154." The federal government granted the NPRR a construction subsidy of alternating sections of unclaimed land forty miles to either side of the tracks along its entire route. The railroad sold the land on its own terms and used the proceeds to finance construction. The railroad company chose where its stations would be built, therefore dictating the locations of towns along the route and determining which individuals made money. Profits from the subsidy were occasionally boosted by surveying the line so that valuable mineral outcrops or timber stands fell within the grant. Other transcontinental railroads were built under similar grants, but never on this scale.

33. Articles of incorporation dated March 24, 1884, Incorporations file 264, Montana Secretary of State's office, Helena, Mont. The incorporation was effective April 1, a week later. Officers are listed in *Gallatin Valley Gazetteer* (1892), 58. Other individuals participating in later purchases by the MRSC or partners include R. Hugh Sawyer and Charles Hugonin.

34. Mortgage deeds, various dates, 4:584, 13:217, 13:221, 13:213, 13:219, 13:223, Gallatin County Clerk and Recorder's Office, Bozeman, Mont.

35. Trust declaration, May 15, 1884, Miscellaneous books 2:365, Gallatin County Clerk and Recorder's Office.

36. The house and ranch James bought were popularly known as the "Culver place." *Avant Courier (Bozeman, Mont.),* March 14, 1889. According to records in the Gallatin County Clerk and Recorder's Office, John A. Culver owned and lived on the property immediately *south* of this quarter section, having assumed an original claim staked by W. W. Jones (Occupancy registration dated July 24, 1865, Miscellaneous C:153).

37. Deed dated April 29, 1884, 4:584, Gallatin County Clerk and Recorder's Office. For one year (1874–75) what became the Randall homestead hosted the Gallatin Valley Female Seminary. John and Christiana Culver held the property until defaulting on a mortgage to J. A. Stephens in 1877 (a loan probably connected to the seminary's operation) and lost the parcel, which had been offered as security, in a sheriff's sale. It was purchased by Timothy C. Ward, who sold the quarter section back to Culver the same day (January 8, 1878, Deeds K:338, 340), though no record of an executed deed transfer appears in the land records. Between 1878 and 1883, the property was sold to Henry and Sarah Dodge, who sold it in 1883 to James M. Sweet and Henry R. Bennet (Deed dated May 3, 1883, Deeds 4:586). Sweet sold the property to James Randall the following year (Deed dated April 29, 1884, Deeds 4:584). Culver's unreleased mortgage to Stephens was finally cancelled and the title cleared by court order in 1885, well after Randall had acquired the property (Miscellaneous Records 2:508).

38. Christchurch registration district (Hampshire, England), Marriages 2b:1046, Public Records Office, Kew, England.

39. Passenger manifest for S.S. *Wisconsin,* October 9, 1884, "Passenger Lists of Vessels Arriving at New York, 1820–1897," microfilm reel 480, Records of the U.S. Customs Service, 1820–91, Record Group 36, National Archives.

40. *Avant Courier (Bozeman, Mont.),* July 4, 1889.

41. "Basil Fitz Herbert [*sic*] Randall," 1919 Indian Army List, Oriental and India Office Collections, British Library; Christchurch Registration District, Register of Births 1890, #272, Public Records Office, Kew. James remained in Gallatin County long enough for his annual tax assessment to be recorded. Gallatin County 1890 tax assessment, p. 80, Gallatin County Treasurer's Office, Bozeman, Mont.

42. Gallatin County 1890 tax assessment, p. 64; 1891 tax assessment, p. 80; 1892 tax assessment, p. 107, Gallatin County Treasurer's Office, Bozeman, Mont. Estimates of the firm's assets and economic standing during the time of Isabel's book are difficult to make, as no local tax records existed prior to statehood (November 4, 1889).

43. Tax assessments (1890), p. 64, Gallatin County Treasurer's Office; Deed dated December 30, 1890, 17:577; Indenture dated March 9, 1891, Miscellaneous 5:8, Gallatin County Clerk and Recorder's Office. At its peak the Manhattan Malting Company controlled over 21,000 acres of Gallatin County farmland and bought grain from local growers as well. Its malting operation supplied malted Montana barley to New York's brewery industry until the passage of Prohibition.

44. (London: Sampson Low, Marston & Co., 1901).

45. N/1/541 fd.298, Oriental and India Office Collections, British Library. Basil was an Oxford student like his father and grandfather. He matriculated to New College in 1909 and completed his coursework but was never granted a degree, probably having left to accept his commission (Card register of matriculated members of the University [1881–1931], Oxford University Archives, UR 11/3/5; Undergraduate register 1909–10, UR 2/1 70). Basil married Rena May Heslop at Sialkot, Baluchistan (Pakistan) on October 12, 1922 (N/1/465, fd.202, OIOC). Their son, Richard James Heslop Randall, was born December 5, 1926, in Lahore, India (N/1/498 fd.178, OIOC).

46. Death certificate dated November 12, 1933, Williton Registration District (Somerset), #320, Public Records Office, Kew.

47. John Van Dyke and Ed Zacher, interview by Richard L. Saunders, August 4, 2001.

A Lady's Ranche Life in Montana

1. The Randalls traveled aboard the S.S. *Wisconsin* as First Class Cabin passengers and arrived in New York harbor October 9, 1884. "Passenger Lists of Vessels Arriving at New York, 1820–1897," Records of the U.S. Customs Service (RG36), National Archives.

2. A fashionable light, two-passenger open buggy, usually pulled by a single horse, having its seat designed as a "Stanhope pillar," something like a bench with the sides and back closed by curved wood paneling (usually painted), which wrapped around it from the floor to armrest height.

3. Probably the Washington Park Club, which boasted not only a racetrack but the ballroom and verandah Isabel mentions and extensive gardens as well. It was established in 1883.

4. This may be an allusion to her younger brother, Captain Henry FitzHerbert, who married Mary Wilson, daughter of Eugene Wilson, of a Minneapolis family. "Greaves Family of Beely, Derbyshire, England."

5. Dickinson, North Dakota, really is the Far West, sitting in the eastern slopes of the Black Hills.

6. The French presence stemmed from the Marquis de Mores's attempt to establish a cattle empire in the area that is now Medora, North Dakota, a few miles east of the Montana border. As the cattle boom swelled in 1883, de Mores built a meat-packing plant outside Little Missouri, and a new town that he named for his wife. Medora, Dakota Territory, and de Mores's "Northern Pacific Refrigerated Car Company" attracted a flurry of fortune-seeking livestock investors and adventurers to the area, including a young Theodore Roosevelt. Accused (probably wrongly) of selling tainted products and ultimately unable to compete with the emerging packing industry in Chicago, the plant folded in 1886. D. Jerome Twenton, "The Marquis de Mores and His

Dakota Venture: A Study in Failure," *Journal of the West* 6, no. 4 (1967): 521–34.

7. Randall's sentiments are precisely the emotions Robert Strahorn fostered in his promotional guides written for the Northern Pacific Rail Road and by Olin Wheeler in the annual guides he produced for the line as well, beginning shortly hereafter. "Wonderland" was applied to the entire route of the NPRR; Yellowstone Park sat as the jewel to the route's scenic crown. Chris J. Magoc, *Yellowstone: The Creation and Selling of an American Landscape, 1870–1903* (Albuquerque: University of New Mexico Press, 2001). Despite the hype, not all tourists who actually made the trip were impressed with the route's scenery; cf. Alice Wellington Rollins, *The Three Tetons: A Story of the Yellowstone* (New York: Cassell & Co., 1887), 10–28.

8. The Bozeman Tunnel was bored through the divide to avoid laying rails up a steep slope at the summit or making a deep cut like the one that I-90 now uses across the same site. A temporary track was laid over the summit so that work trains could move while the tunnel was finished. It was so steep that probably only construction-related material moved across it. Regular Pullman coaches could not be brought over the summit. *Bozeman Weekly Chronicle,* April 4, 1883.

9. "Moreland," Matt Alderson noted in one local paper, "has had substantial growth during the summer, and is one of the few towns in Montana that does not seem to have overgrown. A good hotel and feed stable have long been needed in this vicinity by the traveling public, and have been erected the past summer." *Avant Courier (Bozeman, Mont.),* November 20, 1884.

10. Mary E. Flowers, the wife of William D. Flowers, a partner in Randall's stock concern.

11. Battersea was a slum area of east London.

12. "Mr. H—" could be either Everard Heneage or Duncan T. Hunter, an Englishman and a Scot who arrived in the valley the same year as the Randalls (see note 16). James Randall's cousin Henry L. or "Harry" Lowndes may have been the partner in the "Loundes & Reily, meat market" cited in the *Minnesota, Dakota,*

and Montana Gazetteer and Business Directory (Chicago: R. L. Polk, 1886), 1374. He moved to Livingston about 1889 as the MRSC was coming apart and went to Portland to marry Sadie Sumers, an American girl. He and his new wife eventually returned to Livingston and signed the petition to change Moreland's name to Manhattan in 1891. Nothing further is known about them after the couple sold their holdings in Livingston in early 1890. *Daily Enterprise (Livingston, Mont.),* September 21, 1889; Mortgage deeds, August 7, 1889, 5:279, October 19, 1889, 1:553, January 7, 1890, 5:296, Park County Recorder's Office, Livingston, Mont.; Indenture dated March 9, 1891, Miscellaneous 5:8, Gallatin County Clerk and Recorder's Office.

13. The Moreland Hotel was owned and operated by MRSC partner William Flowers.

14. Her hometown of Holdenhurst was a village only slightly larger than Moreland, though it had been in place for several centuries and Moreland was merely a year old. A two-room railroad station, eight houses, a hotel, a post office, a telegraph office, and several small businesses constituted the entire community. By 1886 Moreland's population stood at forty-five. *Gazetteer and Business Directory* (1886), 1374.

15. Exmoor ponies are probably the oldest and purest native English breed, direct descendants of the horses that wandered into Britain during the last Ice Age. They are comparably small horses, always brown with black points. J. G. and M. G. Speed, *The Exmoor Pony: Its Origins and Characteristics* (Countrywide Livestock, 1977).

16. Almost the same year that James Randall made his first foray west, the Gallatin saw at least one other English group invest in the area. John A. Chater (b. 1856) was a solicitor (lawyer) born in Acton, Cheshire, who hailed from London (1881 Census [Britain] for London, Middlesex). His partners included Everard Henry Fieschi Heneage (b. 1860 in Hemel Hempstead, Hertfordshire [FamilySearch Ancestral File entry under name]), Duncan T. Hunter (b. 1863; Joaquin Miller, *An Illustrated History of the State of Montana* [Chicago: Lewis Publishing, 1894], 184–85), and

Frederick Amcotts (see note 60). All were in their mid- to late twenties. These four acquired a town site and approximately six thousand acres on the Three Forks of the Missouri. They bought up the Bridgeville town site registered by A. W. Paul and Michael Hanley, which included a number of bridges, a small hotel, and other improvements. Since the Chater combination constitutes a separate story and is not central to this book, I have not documented its history, but a historical outline drawn primarily from newspapers (subject to many transcription errors) can be found in *Headwaters Heritage History* (Three Forks, Mont.: Three Forks Area Historical Society, 1983), 324–29. Many writers addressing this part of the Gallatin Valley's history have wrongly assumed that some of the English emigrants were nobility, and a few have erroneously appended titles to the names of various characters. In fact, no title by grant or descent can be confirmed in standard, contemporary sources on the peerage or barontage for any of the Gallatin Valley's known English characters. The popular stories about the wild English expatriates related in newspapers and recounted in local histories may be based more in faulty memory or folklore than fact. All of these accounts are reminiscences; not a word about such exploits appears in contemporary Bozeman newspapers or other sources.

17. True prairie chickens are not native to the Gallatin Valley. What Isabel describes is more likely a sharp-tailed grouse (*Tympanuchus phasianellus*).

18. Undoubtedly. In this situation, correct social manners would have compelled Isabel to help the other women serve or at least have offered to help. She may not have remembered looking down her English nose, but that was probably the perception she left with the ladies of the house.

19. In addition to promotional propaganda, life in the West as a "succession of stirring adventures" is precisely the interpretation that popular literature presented to European and American readers. Characterized by the yellow-backed adventure novels of Beadle & Adams, with titles like "Solid Sam, the Boy Road-Agent; or The Branded Brows, a Tale of Wild Wyoming," they appealed

to urban readers with fantastic plots, stock characters, melodramatic pluck-and-luck action, and typically more plot twists than a skein of yarn.

20. Many other writers commented similarly; cf. William Shepherd, *Prairie Experiences in Handling Cattle and Sheep* (1885; reprint, Freeport, N.Y.: Books for Libraries Press, [1971]), 72.

21. "The major adjustment that any upper class Englishman in the West had to make," notes Athern, "was to accept absolute social equality." Athern, *Westward the Briton,* 79. The visits related in these letters evidently set the stage for the balance of her stay in the Gallatin. That Isabel committed them to print was perhaps one of the reasons she was later honored with the poem that appeared in the *Avant Courier* (see epilogue).

22. Buffalo berry (*Shepherdia argentea*) is common to the eastern Rocky Mountain foothills and plains. It is a tough, thorny shrub that averages eight to ten feet high, favoring bottomlands and stream banks. It survives well where other brushy species might not stand a chance. The berries provide food for numerous birds and mammals (and make good jams, as well), while its spiny branches provide escape cover for a variety of birds and rabbits. Bob Krumm, *Rocky Mountain Berry Book* (Helena, Mont.: Falcon Press, 1991).

23. Short-tailed weasel (*Mustela erminea*), or ermine, which she saw in its winter coat. During the summer the animal is cloaked in chocolate brown with a creamy belly and chest. Montana's chipmunk species, related to *Eutamias minimus,* or least chipmunk, together make it one of the most widely dispersed mammals in North America.

24. The Three Forks ranch to which she refers is not the present community of the same name, but Chater's holdings at the "old town" that occupied a site near the Three Forks of the Missouri where the Gallatin, Madison, and Jefferson Rivers combine. The hotel Isabel mentions is pictured in a bucolic illustration for Michael A. Leeson, *History of Montana, 1739–1885* (Chicago: Warner, Beers & Co., 1885), 1126. To arrive, the Randalls would have followed the road approximately northwest along the Gallatin

through Moreland and Logan to cross the river bridges at least once. The forks of the Missouri were already significant. It was near the fork of the Madison that John Coulter made his famous run from the Blackfeet in 1808 (John Bradbury, *Travels in the Interior of America, in the Years 1809, 1810, and 1811* [Liverpool: printed for the author by Smith and Galway, and published by Sherwood, Neely, and Jones, London, 1817], 17–21). Only a few years later the land between the Jefferson and Madison Rivers became the site for a stockade, one of the earliest fur-trade forts in the Far West, established in 1810 by Peter Menard for the Missouri Fur Company (Thomas James, *Three Years Among the Indians and Mexicans,* ed. Milo Quaife [New York: Citadel Press, 1966], 54–55). In the 1860s the area hosted two boomtowns of the same name (Gallatin and Gallatin City) but on opposite banks of the river. The first was established on the river's west bank, but the entire city moved to a better situation on the east bank. A photo by F. Jay Haynes, H-890, survives in the Montana Historical Society collection. The latter "town" survived only a short time before being abandoned.

25. Northern or greater sage grouse (*Centrocercus urophasianus*), one of the largest birds on the plains. Once very successful on the open plains, today its numbers are declining rapidly due to habitat loss.

26. The Canada goose (*Branta canadensis*) has eleven subspecies, of which the lesser Canada goose is by far the most successful. Which variety Isabel saw cannot be determined.

27. Common cottonwood varieties in the region include *Populus angustifolia* (narrow-leaf cottonwood) and *P. balsamifera ssp. trichocarpa* (black cottonwood).

28. This is probably a sourdough starter, a mixture of flour, water, and sugar, which serves as a medium for airborne natural yeast to ferment. As long as a cook continues to add flour, water, and a bit of sugar, the starter is self-perpetuating and can be tapped for years.

29. Given her genteel upbringing, Isabel was probably unaware that she might have had all the butter she desired simply

by shaking the cream skimmed from the milk. She did learn, but her attempts were satirized by the "Rustic Artiste" in 1889 (see epilogue).

30. Since Bozeman supported a brewery at the time, Spieth & Krug, it is tempting to wonder if this lager was a local product. *Minnesota, Dakota, and Montana Gazetteer and Business Directory* (Chicago: R. L. Polk, 1884), 1162.

31. Frank matriculated to Oxford's Keble College in 1877, but he evidently came west with his brother James rather than complete his college degree. *Alumni Oxonienses: The Members of the University of Oxford, 1715–1886* (London: J. Foster, 1888), 1173.

32. As she notes it here, Isabel's memory must be faulty. Her "Latin" phrase is nonsensical, and the uninflected Greek she inserts seems to be the same.

33. Springtails, or snow fleas (*Achorutes nivicola*), are not fleas at all. They feed on decaying plant matter year-round but are especially visible popping around atop the snow beneath trees during sunny late-winter days.

34. Given as "F—" in the text, this is probably, but not certainly, Mary E. Flowers, William Flowers's wife.

35. The first true pheasants had been introduced to Oregon from China only one year earlier. The birds probably did not arrive in Montana for another three decades. What Isabel describes is probably a ruffed grouse (*Bonasa umbellus*), once one of the most widely dispersed game birds in North America. It thrives in harsh-winter areas.

36. William Flowers, one of the Moreland Ranch Stock Company partners, received a load of hogs from the East the previous autumn and had farmed them out to one of the other characters in the MRSC concern. *Avant Courier (Bozeman, Mont.),* November 20, 1884.

37. This may be Dr. William Tracy, a Three Forks resident. *Avant Courier (Bozeman, Mont.),* December 18, 1884.

38. Moreland Ranch Stock Company.

39. "Short brown grass" could identify any number of highly nutritious bunch grasses native to the North American plains

between Canada and Mexico, including *Buchloe dactyloides,* or buffalo grass.

40. While Isabel may have seen a white-tailed jackrabbit (*Lepus townsendii*), which may have been the prairie subspecies (*L.t. campanius*), it is more likely that she saw a snowshoe hare (*L. americanus)* in winter coat.

41. James and Isabel lived about a mile above the confluence where Camp Creek joins the Gallatin River. At this point the Gallatin river bottoms are about a quarter of a mile wide. The Gallatin flows along the eastern bluff, Camp Creek today flows roughly down the center, but the whole area is threaded by small streams and rills. The Randall property straddled Camp Creek.

42. The black-billed magpie (*Pica pica*), which plagued the Lewis & Clark company in 1804, still robs camps and picnics throughout the West.

43. Probably the American robin (*Turdus migratorius*), which is quite common throughout Montana. The other is probably the mountain bluebird (*Sialia currucoides*), which exhibits the same patterns of occupancy in the Gallatin Valley today.

44. This reference to a solar eclipse fixes a positive point for calculating dates within Isabel's narrative, despite a minor discrepancy in either the editing or the original letter (which has not been located and may not survive). Modern astronomic calculations date the annular solar eclipse Isabel witnessed to March 16, 1885, one week earlier than the March 23 date appearing in the book. Statistics for the event were calculated for NASA as: Saros #118, gamma .803, eclipse magnitude .978, duration 01m55s, latitude 48.9 north, longitude 106.1 west, 36 altitude, path width 132km. Eclipse table/predictions courtesy of Fred Espenak, NASA/Goddard Space Flight Center.

45. The "South Kensington" book to which she refers is likely the text for a cooking school located in this west-central London neighborhood, Rose Owen Cole's *The Official Handbook for the National Training School for Cookery: Containing the Lessons on Cookery Which Constitute the Course of Instruction in the School* (London, 1877). An American edition edited by

Thomas K. Chambers and Eliza A. Youmans appeared the following year under the title *Lessons in Cookery* (New York: D. Appleton and Company, 1878).

46. "A. W. Paul of Three Forks was unfortunate with a shipment of horses sent East over the [Northern Pacific] last week. He started with two car loads, but on reaching Moreland eighteen head were found to be dead, having got down and been trampled upon." Paul claimed that the animals were down before the train left the Three Forks station and that officials refused to compromise the train schedule by taking time to uncouple and sidetrack his car. (*Avant Courier,* December 4, 1884). Swine are omnivores and will not hesitate to feed on the carcasses of nearly any animal—including their own young.

47. The brook, brown, and rainbow trouts now common to area streams are introduced species. Isabel's table fare more probably consisted of Montana arctic grayling (*Thymallus arcticus montanus*), which is native to the upper Missouri River. This fish does not coexist well with trout species except for native cutthroat trout, suggesting that the trout mentioned were native westslope cutthroat (*Oncorhynchus clarki lewisi*). The whitefish were probably mountain whitefish (*Prosopium williamsoni*).

48. Isabel calls her servant's language unintelligible by alluding to the Greek origin of the word "barbaric." The Dorian invasion of Acadian Greece in the nineteenth century BCE was by those who did not speak Greek, and whose language simply sounded nonsensical, like "ba-ba-ba-ba," or as we might say today, "blah-blah-blah." The Dorians were therefore "ba-ba"-rians, a title that entered English usage as identifying merely the uncultured.

49. *infra dignitatem*—beneath one's dignity. Hugh Percy Jones, *Dictionary of Foreign Phrases and Classical Quotations,* new ed. (Edinburgh: John Grant, 1963), 57.

50. A poem written in the mid-nineteenth century by G. J. Whyte-Melville, which enjoyed a popularity in British equestrian circles and was incorporated in Rudyard Kipling's short story "Route of the White Hussars." The complete lyric can be found in *The Poetry of Horses,* ed. Olwen Way (London: J. A. Allen, 1994).

"Annie Laurie" is one of Scotland's best-loved songs, written as a poem in the opening years of the eighteenth century by William Douglas of Fingland in praise of a daughter of Sir Robert Laurie, 1st baronet Maxwelton. It has many variations and was set to many different tunes. The tune most closely identified with the song was written in the mid-nineteenth century by Alicia Spottiswoode (Lady John Scott).

51. The untitled song is "sung" by the title character in Sir Walter Besant's *Uncle Jack, etc.* ([London: Chatto & Windus, 1885], 49–50), a book which would have been a new release at this time. An American edition was published the same year under the title, *Uncle Jack and Other Stories* (New York: Harper & Bros., 1885).

52. Probably a rendition of a sheet-music song popular during his childhood, "The Bicester Hunt Galop" (Cheltenham, England: Edward Hale & Co. [1860?]), written anonymously under the pseudonym "Minnie."

53. Notice here she uses a term to identify herself and her station that she had earlier chided Americans for using too loosely.

54. Her description is too vague to allow identification.

55. At home the FitzHerberts and virtually all other English dwellings would have been burning coal, which leaves cinders or "ashes" akin to sand and gravel.

56. A generic term for apples sliced and preserved by drying for winter use. *Webster's Revised Unabridged Dictionary,* 1913.

57. Though thousands of Chinese immigrants lived in Montana during the territorial period, typically as migrants who followed placer mining and the railroad, they are almost transparent, leaving no records of their own and being virtually ignored in the newspapers and other public documents. Virginia City, about fifty miles from Moreland, had a large Chinese population through the 1870s that dispersed only after reworking tailings from the placer-mining boom and removal of the territorial capital to Helena.

58. Many flower varieties, particularly from the *Erigeron* genus, fit her brief description of "ox-eyed daisies," but only two

local species, *Opuntia fragilis* and/or *O. polycantha,* are likely identities for Isabel's cactus. For her generic "violet" the *Viola* genus provides hundreds of possible species, of which the Canada violet (*V. canadensis*) is probably the most likely for the region. The term "Lenten lily" is often applied indiscriminately to any early-blooming lily. Isabel's was perhaps *Erythronium grandiflorum,* the yellow glacier lily or yellow dogtooth violet, a common spring ephemeral.

59. The Shire breed originated in the "English Great Horse" and was bred as a combat platform for medieval knights. It counts ancestors brought to Britannia by the Romans and muscular Low Country stock (Belgians) carried to eastern England. By the 1600s the Shire had been bred into a powerful draft animal suitable for farmwork and heavy hauling. It remains the largest, heaviest horse breed. Walter Gilbey, *Concise History of the Shire Horse,* 2nd ed. (Liss, England: Spur Publications Co., 1976). A stud of this type suggests that the Randalls were primarily breeding workhorses, not the polo or riding stock typically identified with English investor/emigrants in the West.

60. Though given in Isabel's book as "A—," this and subsequent references are probably to a partner in the Hanley-Paul buyout at Three Forks "old town" and the only Englishman in the area known to have a surname beginning with *A,* Frederick Augustus Cracroft-Amcotts. Amcotts (1853–97) resigned an officer's commission in the Fifth Dragoon Guards Regiment to come to Montana. The census enumerator listed him erroneously as "Frederic A. E. Amcotts" (1881 Census [Britain] for Caythorpe, Lincolnshire County; International Genealogical Index entry). *Headwaters Heritage History* cites his given name as both "Frederic" and "Andrew" in various places.

61. Wild rose would be either the prickly rose (*Rosa acicularis*) or the Woods rose (*R. woodsii*); the single sunflower could be a cutleaf coneflower (*Rudbeckia laciniata*) or possibly a western coneflower (*R. occidentalis*), though there are other possibilities as well.

62. Harry Lowndes.

63. Possibly a jab at her two youngest sisters, Rachel and Edith, who were still at home.

64. "Holland" is a lightweight linen cloth, heavier than muslin, which was originally a product of the Low Countries. It was frequently used for summer clothing. "Habit" refers to any formal riding outfit, which possessed a distinct style in British equestrian circles and was typically woolen, except for the plain "country" habit. A typical habit consisted of a riding skirt that hung on the left (or near) side to the length of the spur. On the right or off side the skirt was much longer. When dismounted, the skirt was buttoned high on the waistline to even up its hemline. Under the skirt a woman wore long trousers with a strap or knee trousers and stockings with a gaiter. The blouse was more like a jacket cut and fitted to hang down to the saddle; by the 1880s fashion had incorporated a masculine style to habits, with the collar finished off by a cravat. A cylinder hat and veil completed the costume, though Isabel probably wore a broad-brimmed hat of some sort in the United States. Isabel notes that "I never wear a habit at all about home" (p. 97). That can be taken to mean either that she dressed specifically for her frequent saddle trips with James or that she usually wore regular housework clothes to ride. Either would require her to ride an English sidesaddle to accommodate the skirt. It is also possible that she indulged but did not confess to wearing the American curiosity of a "California riding costume"—a divided skirt—with which she could have ridden astride in a common stock saddle. Regrettably, Isabel gives us no clear clues.

65. A small, felt-topped table, like a card table.

66. She does not specify a direction, but the group probably followed the Gallatin River up to the canyon of the same name. They may have traveled directly south, across the western end of the Gallatin Valley and into the lower reaches of the Spanish Peaks, which are probably the peaks "capped with glistening white snow" she later describes.

67. Phosphorus-tipped friction match.

68. That is, to tell a tall tale or at least to stretch the truth a little.

69. Clark's Fork is one of the tributary streams that run west and south into northeastern Yellowstone, the valley of which now constitutes the Northeast Entrance, below the Absaroka Range to the south. It is a well-established corridor for grizzly bears moving between Yellowstone and the high country.

70. Undefined slang or expression. May be a reference to awarding a loving-cup trophy for a prize-winning performance—in other words, "enough already, you win."

71. *Populus tremuloides,* or quaking aspen.

72. *Cervus canadensis,* or elk.

73. The western rattlesnake (*Crotalus viridis*) is Montana's only venomous snake. If she reports accurately, the size Isabel describes suggests that it was a very old critter and not the distinctly smaller subspecies, the prairie rattlesnake (*C.v. viridis*).

74. Master of ceremonies, today colloquially written "emcee."

75. Surely in this Isabel misremembers the name, for the demise is not cited in any Bozeman newspapers around this time.

76. Though presented in her book as "G—," the familiarity she demonstrates suggests this is most likely Godfrey FitzHerbert (1864–), the fourth of the six FitzHerbert children and Isabel's youngest brother.

77. The combination of cold fog and coal smoke from countless urban chimneys was responsible for many of the respiratory problems common to European cities. Montana was widely touted for its clean, dry air, which did allow coughs due to airborne particulates to clear up; cf. McElrath, *Yellowstone Valley,* intro.

78. Isabel quotes the first two lines of a well-known lyric by Charles Mackay, which came from a popular musical number that English composer Henry Russell inserted in a stage production called *The Emigrant's Progress; or, Life in the Far West.* It appeared first in text only in the *Musical Bouquet Edition: Copyright Collection of the Songs, Scenas, &c., &c., of H. Russell* (London: Musical Bouquet, [1855?]), 56–57, and with the music in an edition done the following year as the *Musical Bouquet Edition: One Hundred Songs by H. Russell* (London, 1856), no. 7. The lyric

encapsulates the ideals fueling British interest in the American West, particularly the final verse:

> To the west! to the west! there is wealth to be won,
> The forest to clear is the work to be done:
> Where the stars and the stripes like a banner unfurled,
> Invites to its regions the world, all the world.
>
> Where the people are true to the vows that they frame,
> And their pride is the honor that's shown to their name;
> Away! far away! let us hope for the best,
> And build up a home in the land of the west.

79. This surely may have happened, but it and similar stories have been told so widely and attributed to so many different places that the tale can only be said to have passed into the realm of folklore, even in Isabel's day.

80. This was probably Rudolf Vogel and Frederick Buchler's establishment on Main Street, the only business in town that advertised both an eatery and rooms. *Minnesota, Dakota, and Montana Gazetteer and Business Directory* (1884), 1163.

81. A statement later worthy of Marxist diatribe. The English gentry considered "tradesmen" as distinctly lower-class individuals, whereas in the United States economic position represented power and position. What Bozeman residents regarded as merely a polite overture to business was a subject for Isabel's amazement, since she would have reserved the formality of a handshake and greeting for a social equal.

82. These were the days before heeled cowboy boots were popular among women. The heel of the boot keeps a foot from slipping entirely through a stirrup, reducing the risk of a rider's being dragged by the leg over the ground if thrown from the saddle. The "slipper stirrup" common to women's side saddles began to be replaced with safer quick-release stirrups in the 1880s. These unlatched and allowed a tangled foot to drop out, which prevented one from being dragged.

83. Thomas H. Carroll, Charles M. Chambliss, Henry W. Foster, J. McC. Lansing, John M. Waters, and Robert M. Whitefoot were listed as Bozeman physicians in the *Minnesota, Dakota and Montana Gazetteer and Business Directory* (1886). She would have been seen by one of them.

84. One pound sterling plus one shilling, or a sum equivalent to about fifteen dollars at the time.

85. A *chinook* is a warm westerly wind than can come up suddenly and clear several inches of standing snow in a day. Isabel invokes the widely held and entirely groundless belief, promoted by shameless propagandist William Gilpin, that rainfall would increase over arid regions in direct response to settlement and cultivation. The subject is addressed summarily in Henry Nash Smith, *Virgin Land: The American West as Symbol and Myth* (Cambridge, Mass.: Harvard University Press, 1950), ch. 16, and is treated at length by the same author in "Rain Follows the Plow: The Notion of Increased Rainfall for the Great Plains, 1844–1880," *Huntington Library Quarterly* 10 (February 1947): 169–83.

86. In the 1885 election the Conservative party won control of Parliament from the liberal Labor party of Prime Minister William Gladstone. The election results set the stage for the first meaningful parliamentary discussion of Irish sovereignty, which Gladstone hoped to resolve before leaving office. George Shaw-Lefevre Eversley, *Gladstone and Ireland: The Irish Policy of Parliament from 1850–1894* (Westport, Conn.: Greenwood Press, [1971]).

87. Paraffin oil is a mineral oil similar to kerosene (coal oil) but has no odor when burned. As clear as water but oily, it is today used primarily for ornamental candles.

88. This was probably hired from M. T. Barney. An 1886 photo of this livery stable in Three Forks survives in the F. Jay Haynes collection, H-1721, Montana Historical Society, Helena.

89. The Gallatin bridge can be seen in a photo by F. J. Haynes published in *Headwaters Heritage History,* 54.

90. Horses are measured from ground to whithers (top of the shoulders) in "hands" of four inches. Fourteen hands equals fifty-six inches. The English weight measurement of "stone"

varies from 6 to 24 pounds; the official measure came in at 14 pounds. The load of rider, tack, and bags described here would have come to 196 pounds.

91. That is, good only to pull horse-drawn trolleys.

92. Isabel here refers to the question of Irish self-rule and British politics in the wake of the 1885 election. Liberal prime minister William Gladstone introduced his first Home Rule Bill in 1886. The bill would have established a separate Irish legislature while reserving many powers to the British Parliament at Westminster, including taxation. The bill did not pass. The incoming Conservative government rejected effectual Irish independence and instead adopted a policy of land reform in hopes of salving Irish complaints. That measure set the stage for the civil war of the 1910s. Eversley, *Gladstone and Ireland,* 258–317.

93. Isabel here distinguishes between the early western stock saddle of Mexican extraction and the English riding saddle familiar to most of her British readers; cf. Richard E. Ahlborn, ed., *Man Made Mobile: Early Saddles of Western North America* (Washington, D.C.: Smithsonian Institution Press, 1980).

94. Isabel departed Moreland hastily. From the variety of data she includes and the fact that she uses past tense in virtually all of the sentences, this letter is likely a compilation or rewrite made from several other letters or may have been one written from memory specifically for the edited edition.

95. The lease must have been an informal agreement, as the contract was not registered with the county. The terms are unknown.

Epilogue

1. Isabella Bird, *A Lady's Life in the Rocky Mountains,* 3rd American ed. (New York: G. P. Putnam, 1886).

2. Elizabeth Hampsten, *Read This Only to Yourself: The Private Writings of Midwestern Women, 1880–1910* (Bloomington: Indiana University Press, 1982), 48–95.

3. Deed dated May 25, 1887, 15:348; Deeds dated January 27, 1888, and February 1, 1888, 15:391, 15:393, Gallatin County Clerk and Recorder's Office.

4. *Avant Courier (Bozeman, Mont.),* March 14, 1889.

5. After being identified as the author of her book, Isabel began avoiding townsfolk and neighbors.

6. This is a biting comment both on Isabel's swarthy complexion and on her pride about her cooking skills, as displayed in her book. Since a pale, untanned face was a mark of genteel culture, proving that one did not have to work outdoors, the Rustic Artiste jabs at Isabel by suggesting she cover her tan with flour instead of the face powder she sees on her neighbors. She (or he) is saying that Isabel could demonstrate that she was a real lady by taking more time to practice her domestic skills—basically, "stay at home rather than ride idly around the countryside," which was a mark of the English gentry.

7. Sally Brass was a sallow character from Charles Dickens's *Old Curiosity Shop.* A description of her can be found in chapter 33 of that book. It may have been exceedingly uncharitable of the Rustic Artiste to invoke such a comparison but demonstrates the depth of anger Isabel's neighbors felt about what she said of them in her book.

8. *Avant Courier (Bozeman, Mont.),* April 25, 1889. In "Isabelle Randall and the 'Natives,'" *Montana: Magazine of Western History* 52, no. 1 (spring 2002), Phyllis Smith identifies the 'Rustic Artiste' as Aline Anceney Howard but cites no source to substantiate the claim.

9. Zincke, *Last Winter,* 230.

10. Mortgage deed, May 24, 1889, 5:510, Gallatin County Clerk and Recorder's Office.

11. *Avant Courier (Bozeman, Mont.),* June 20, 1889.

12. "Middle Creek," *Avant Courier (Bozeman, Mont.),* June 20, 1889.

13. Claims by J. Lowndes Randall and William Flowers dated October 30, 1889, Water claims 2:157, 2:158, Gallatin County Clerk

and Recorder's Office. The Randalls had probably departed for England by the time Flowers registered an amendment to the second claim on December 24, 1889, which only he signed. From Chichester, Sussex, in 1891 the Randalls signed over water rights that had been missed in earlier deeds. Deed dated May 11, 1891, Deeds 19:301 and Water deeds 2:114, Gallatin County Clerk and Recorder's Office.

14. The Randall's counsel, R. Hugh Sawyer, signed a sale deed for them a year later (deed dated December 27, 1890, 17:577) and then must have thought better of it. From Bristol, Hampshire, the Randalls themselves signed another sale deed to Henry Altenbrand on January 21, 1891 (deed dated January 2, 1891, Deeds 18:41, Gallatin County Clerk and Recorder's Office). See pp. 30–34 for a discussion of their postdeparture lives. James's cousin Harry Lowndes and his American wife sold their town lots in Livingston a few months later (deed dated January 7, 1890, 5:296, Park County Clerk and Recorder's Office).

Index